Those who write off Israel's exile as a stagnant time, largely irrelevant to theology without a message to the modern church and world, should read this book. Both a scholar and a pastor, Bergquam is diligent in his research and passionate about God's plan. The numerous initial questions about renewal and fulfillment will intrigue, and so will the careful sorting out of answers that follow. The theme of promise and fulfillment, often discussed on the large canvas of OT and NT, is here profiled on a smaller canvas, but still in brilliant colors. The discussion ranges between the pre-exilic/exilic prophets Ezekiel and Jeremiah and the later books of Haggai, Zechariah, Ezra and Nehemiah. Bergquam overturns Wellhausen's negative assessment of the exile, distills the insights of other scholars, writes with clarity, and with a gift for synthesis, keeps readers on track with frequent summaries. An edifying read.

Elmer Martens

# The Babylonian Experience and Israel's Future

## Promise and Fulfillment

Paul Stephen Bergquam

CROSSBOOKS
PUBLISHING

# CONTENTS

# ACKNOWLEDGEMENTS

This work is dedicated to the memory of Joyce Friedemann, a delightful Christian lady who constantly encouraged me to press on and not lose heart, especially during those dark days when progress was slow and there seemed to be no end in sight.

Second, I want to thank Dr. Elmer Martens and his lovely wife, Phyllis.

Dr. Martens has been both a mentor and a friend. His patience, insights, and guidance have proved invaluable. Phyllis Martens and Stacy Ross have provided exceptional editing assistance. Also, my wife, Cherry, has helped by giving her insights into the proper use of the English language.

Third I want to thank the staff of Trinity Presbyterian Church, family, and friends for all of their help and encouragement. Additionally, the staff at Fresno Pacific Library has assisted and guided me as I have searched for information and materials relevant to this study.

Finally, I want to thank my Heavenly Father for His grace and mercy in my life. He has continued to teach me the truth of Isa. 55:8, "'For my thoughts are not your thoughts, neither are your ways my ways,' says *Adonai*."

# PREFACE

This book developed from a dissertation project at Trinity Seminary in Newburgh, Indiana. For a number of years I have been interested in Israel in Old Testament prophecy and God's end-time plan for Israel. This interest goes back to my time at Dallas Seminary. Over the years, while a number of my Christian colleagues have concluded that God has abandoned his original plan for Israel, Romans 9-11 has anchored me in the belief that God has unfinished business with his ancient people. Throughout her history Israel has often rebelled against God's authority and sought to be autonomous from him. And yet, God has not only faithfully kept his promises but has always maintained a remnant of Jewish believers.

My interest in Israel in prophecy was piqued by God's specific promises made to Israel in passages like Jeremiah 31 & 33. In these chapters, God's heart is stirred not only for Israel as a whole, but specifically for Ephraim, the house of Judah, and the house of Israel. Then, near the end of chapter 31 God speaks of his decrees concerning the sun, moon, stars, and waves of the sea. He concludes with these words: "Only if these decrees vanish from my sight," declares the Lord, "will the descendants of Israel ever cease to be a nation before me" (v. 36). God promises to maintain national Israel.

For centuries this promise seemed irrelevant and an impossible dream for a scattered people. Then in 1948, the dream suddenly became reality. The nation of Israel once again appeared on the stage of history. Can Israel today survive? Yes, but only because of God's unfailing promises. Her calling is be a source of joy and blessing to the world (Gen 12:1-3).

# Abbreviations

| | |
|---|---|
| *AJSL* | *American Journal of Semitic Languages and Literature* |
| *ALB* | *Archaeology of the Land of the Bible.* **Ephraim Stern. The Anchor Bible Reference Library 11. New York, 2001** |
| *AUSS* | *Andrews University Seminary Studies* |
| *BAIAS* | *Bulletin of the Anglo-Israel Archaeological Society* |
| *BA* | *Biblical Archaeologist* |
| *BAR* | *Biblical Archaeological Review* |
| *Bib* | *Biblica* |
| *BibInt* | *Biblical Interpretation* |
| *BSac* | *Bibliotheca Sacra* |
| *BSOS* | *Bulletin of the School of Oriental Studies* |
| *BT* | *The Bible Translator* |
| *BTB* | *Biblical Theology Bulletin* |
| *CBQ* | *Catholic Biblical Quarterly* |
| *CTJ* | *Calvin Theological Journal* |
| *CTR* | *Criswell Theological Review* |
| *CurBR* | *Currents in Biblical Research* |
| *CurTM* | *Currents in Theology and Mission* |
| *Dir* | *Direction* |
| *Enc* | *Encounter* |

| | |
|---|---|
| *ETL* | *Ephemerides theologicae lovanienses* |
| *Evan* | *Evangel* |
| *EvQ* | *Evangelical Quarterly* |
| *EvRT* | *Evangelical Review of Theology* |
| *ExpTim* | *Expository Times* |
| *Heb* | *Hebraica* |
| *HTR* | *Harvard Theological Review* |
| *HUCA* | *Hebrew Union College Annual* |
| *Int* | *Interpretation* |
| *IR* | *Illif Review* |
| *JAOS* | *Journal of the American Oriental Society* |
| *JATS* | *Journal of the Adventist Theological Society* |
| *JBL* | *Journal of Biblical Literature* |
| *JBQ* | *Jewish Bible Quarterly* |
| *JETS* | *Journal of the Evangelical Theological Society* |
| *JJTP* | *Journal of Jewish Thought and Philosophy* |
| *JNES* | *Journal of Near Eastern Studies* |
| *JR* | *Journal of Religion* |
| *JSJ* | *Journal for the Study of Judaism* |
| *JSNT* | *Journal for the Study of the New Testament* |
| *JSOT* | *Journal for the Study of the Old Testament* |
| **JSOTSup** | Journal for the Study of the Old Testament: Supplement Series |
| **MT** | **Masoretic Text** |
| *NEA* | *Near Eastern Archaeology* |
| *NIB* | *The New Interpreter's Bible* |

| *NIV* | *New International Version* |
| *NIDOTTE* | *New International Dictionary of Old Testament Theology and Exegesis.* Edited by W. A. VanGemeren. 5 vols. Grand Rapids, 1997 |
| *OHBW* | *The Oxford History of the Biblical World.* Edited by Michael D. Coogan. New York, 1998 |
| *Pneuma* | *Pneuma: Journal for the Society of Pentecostal Studies* |
| *PRSt* | *Perspectives in Religious Studies* |
| *PSB* | *Princeton Seminary Bulletin* |
| *RB* | *Revue Biblique* |
| *RelSRev* | *Religious Studies Review* |
| *RevBL* | *Review of Biblical Literature* |
| *RevExp* | *Review and Expositor* |
| *RevQ* | *Revue de Qumran* |
| *RTR* | *Reformed Theological Review* |
| *Sem* | *Semitica* |
| *SJOT* | *Scandinavian Journal of the Old Testament* |
| *SJT* | *Scottish Journal of Theology* |
| *Them* | *Themelios* |
| *ThTo* | *Theology Today* |
| *TWOT* | *Theological Wordbook of the Old Testament.* Edited by R. Laird Harris. Chicago, 1980 |
| *TynBul* | *Tyndale Bulletin* |
| *VT Vetus* | *Testamentum* |
| *WTJ* | *Westminster Theological Journal* |
| *ZAW* | *Zeitschrift für die Alttestamentliche Wissenschaft* |

# Chapter 1

# Toward a New Understanding of the Early Persian Period

The goal of this study is to provide a new framework for understanding the Babylonian captivity and the early Persian period that followed. For well over a century, this era has been portrayed as a prophetically insignificant age marked by lifeless ritualism. This negative assessment gained widespread acceptance in the late nineteenth century, largely through the writings of the German scholar Julius Wellhausen.[1]

Wellhausen equated Second Temple Judaism with medieval Catholicism. In his words postexilic Judaism was "intimately allied to the old Catholic church, which was in fact its child."[2] He associated the worst of medieval Catholicism, its ritual and lifeless ceremony, with his depiction of Second Temple Judaism.

---

[1]  Wellhuasen's influence extended to the Encyclopedia Britannica in an age where the written word was considered nearly infallible!

[2]  Julius Wellhausen, *Prolegomena to the History of Israel* (Atlanta: Scholars Press, 1994), 402.

According to Wellhausen, the Book of Deuteronomy was the book of the law found in the temple during King Josiah's reign. From this, Wellhausen concluded that this book served as the catalyst that led to the development of postexilic Judaism, which he portrayed as functionally formal and spiritually dead. In comparing the pre- and postexilic eras he said, "At first it was naïve, and what was chiefly considered was the quantity and quality of the gifts; afterwards it became legal,—the scrupulous fulfillment of the law, that is, of the prescribed ritual, was what was looked to before everything."[3]

According to Wellhausen's model, the exile set the stage for Second Temple Judaism. He believed that Ezekiel's influence was primarily to prepare conditions for the "monarchy of the high priest."[4] To quote Wellhausen, "The hierocracy towards which Ezekiel had already opened the way was simply inevitable."[5]

Professor Michael Floyd summarizes Wellhausen's portrayal of the postexilic era as a period of theological, social, and spiritual decline. Floyd points to four major characteristics surfacing from Wellhausen's view of the Second Temple period:

1) profound theological disappointment resulting from Judah's failure to regain national independence and restore the Davidic monarchy; 2) degeneration and loss of vitality resulting from the centralization of the cult of Yahweh in Jerusalem and its dissociation from local holy places; 3) loss of critical spirit resulting from the decline of prophecy; and 4) priestly legalism resulting from theocratic

---

3    Ibid., 61.
4    Wellhausen, *Prolegomena*, 495.
5    Ibid.

authority given to Jerusalem's temple establishment by Judah's imperial overlords.[6]

While there were undoubtedly serious problems and challenges that surfaced during the postexilic era (see Hag. 2:10-14; Mal. 1:6-2:16), this author believes that the weight of biblical, historical, and archaeological evidence points to a very different and clearly more nuanced understanding of the Second Temple era than the simplistic one portrayed by Wellhausen. In particular, Wellhausen failed to grasp the multi-faceted impact that the destruction of Jerusalem, and in particular the temple, along with the protracted exile in Babylon played in Israel's history.

A second Biblical scholar, David Hubbard, writing in the early 1980s summarized the early postexilic era in the following terms: "The circumstances in Judah and Jerusalem stood in drab contrast to the preexilic period, let alone to the promised future glory of Isaiah 40-55 and Ezekiel 40-48."[7] Since Hubbard wrote these words, scholars have gained important insight into the Second Temple era, much of which is positive. Like Wellhausen, it seems

---

[6]  Michael H. Floyd, "Zechariah and Changing Views of Second Temple Judaism in Recent Commentaries," *RelSRev* 25 (July 1999): 260. Floyd's important work illustrates how the Wellhausian interpretation followed by the historical-critical family of methods, including source, form, tradition and redaction criticism, has dominated the modern study of the post-exilic prophets, especially Zechariah, throughout the past century. Recently the literary-critical method with its focus on the shape and meaning of the text's present form has challenged Wellhausen's view of the post-exilic period. Unfortunately, deeply embedded ideas like old stumps are not easily removed!

[7]  David A. Hubbard, "Hope in the Old Testament," *TynBul* 34 (1983): 48.

that Hubbard arrived at his conclusions using limited or partial information that appears to have misinformed his conclusions.

Recently, the prominent Biblical scholar, N. T. Wright, described the restoration under Sheshbazzar and Zerubbabel as merely a "geographical return from exile."[8] Like Wellhausen and Hubbard, Wright's assessment of this era is decidedly negative.

Wright's evaluation of the return highlights the following deficiencies. First, he argues that the return lacked the visible manifestation of God's glory that was so much in evidence during the original Exodus and at important moments in First Temple history. Second, Wright finds a lack of prophetic fulfillment, specifically in a "final decisive victory over Israel's enemies."[9] Third, in relation to God's promises made to David, Wright sees no "universally welcomed royal dynasty."[10] Consequently, Wright concludes that in these three areas the return from Babylon failed to meet prophetic expectation. For Wright the exile simply continued.

However, not all scholars agree with the conclusions reached by Wellhausen, Hubbard, and Wright. Professor Michael Floyd states that recent research and archaeological discoveries, including the Dead Sea Scrolls, have contributed to what he describes as

a new and clearer picture of Second Temple Judaism in general. The pattern of religious life taking shape in the restoration no longer appears to fit Wellhausen's description

---

[8]   N. T. Wright, *Jesus and the Victory of God* (Minneapolis: Fortress Press, 1996), 621. Wright's description falls under the rubric of the traditional view.

[9]   Ibid.

[10]   Ibid.

of *Spätjudentum* very well. In general, Second Temple Judaism turns out to have been more richly diverse than he imagined. This revised view of the outcome requires a revised view of the origins of Second Temple Judaism as reflected in documents like Zechariah.[11]

To this, Floyd adds, "Emergent Second Temple Judaism is described as a creative transformation of preexilic religious traditions, in which the continuing vitality of prophecy played an important role and to which Zechariah made a particularly positive theological contribution."[12]

If it can be demonstrated, contra Wellhausen and others, that Second Temple Judaism creatively transformed earlier religious traditions within the boundaries of previous prophecy, then the origins of this period, including people and events that shaped its development, deserve further examination. Two experiences, the Babylonian exile and the return under Sheshbazzar and Zerubbabel, stand out as seminal events that served to shape the Second Temple period.

In particular, the text of Ezekiel anticipates dramatic positive changes taking place in Israel's theology. One example is evidenced in the move away from the generational fatalism that existed in preexilic Israel to a belief system marked by individual responsibility within each generation (see Ezek. 18:1-4, 19-20). Additionally, in combination with a return to the land, Yahweh

---

[11] Floyd, "Zechariah and Changing Views," 260.

[12] Ibid., 261. In the same paragraph Floyd calls the academic community to give serious reflection to whether it may unwittingly still "be using scholarly categories and concepts in which there remains a residue of anti-Judaism."

promised to effect a dynamic spiritual transformation in the hearts of his people. He said,

> I will sprinkle clean water on you, and you will be clean; I will cleanse you from all your impurities and from all your idols. I will give you a new heart and put a new spirit in you; I will remove from you your heart of stone and give you a heart of flesh. And I will put my Spirit in you and move you to follow my decrees and be careful to keep my laws (Ezek. 36:25-27).

This promise is followed by God's pledge to return his blessing to the land in the form of agricultural fruitfulness. This promise is specifically addressed in both Haggai and Zechariah where God removes the curse and returns the land to fruitfulness (see Hag. 2:15-19; Zech. 8:11-12).

## Study Question

How convincing is the evidence for the assertion that God used the Babylonian captivity to initiate a new spiritual work among the exiled remnant? Additionally, can it be demonstrated that God fulfilled preexilic and exilic prophesies in the postexilic era?

The research focus of this study begins with an examination of the promises made by the preexilic/exilic prophets, specifically Jeremiah and Ezekiel. What did these prophets say about Israel's future? Second, what does Scripture and the historical record reveal about the subsequent outworking of these prophecies? As an example, how is one to correlate the promises made in

Jeremiah 24: 5-7 with the historical realities that followed? The text reads,

> This is what the Lord, the God of Israel, says: 'Like these good figs, I regard as good the exiles from Judah, whom I sent away from this place to the land of the Babylonians. My eyes will watch over them for their good, and I will bring them back to this land. I will build them up and not tear them down; I will plant them and not uproot them. I will give them a heart to know me, that I am the Lord. They will be my people, and I will be their God, for they will return to me with all their heart.'

Several important pledges are highlighted in this passage that will need to be explored. First, God expresses his favor toward these exiles, promising to watch over them for their good and bring them back to the land. Second, God says that he will build them up and plant them as opposed to tearing down and uprooting them (compare with Jer. 1:9-10). Third, God promises to implant in these people a heart that knows him as Yahweh, the holy, awesome, covenant-keeping God of Israel. The focus here is upon God's internal work in the hearts of his people.

Fourth, God's promise suggests a new relationship developing between God and his people. This relationship will be something unlike the relationship known in preexilic times. At the same time, this relationship will include the common covenant formula: "They will be my people and I will be their God."

Further, God promised that these people would return to him with an undivided heart. Israel's history was marred by its ongoing attraction to the gods of the surrounding nations.

Yahweh promised that his people would return to him with hearts singularly devoted to him.[13]

In examining the exile and return, can one find evidence that God intervened in a way that brought dynamic and lasting change within the exile community? Both Jeremiah and Ezekiel called God's people to repentance. Is there evidence that the Jews in Babylon turned to Yahweh in repentance and faith (Ezek. 18:30-32)?[14]

Can it be demonstrated that God used the exile experience to mark a new beginning and set a new course for the remnant that eventually returned from Babylon? Also, as suggested above, did Judaism develop in some fundamentally positive ways in this era?

Finally, as one examines the early postexilic era through the texts of Haggai and Zechariah 1-8 and also through Ezra and Nehemiah, what can be concluded in relation to God's larger redemptive program for the Jewish remnant, for greater Israel, and for the nations? For example, did what happened on a small scale among the remnant that returned to the land foreshadow a much grander return promised for Israel at the end of this age?

---

[13] Writing about this passage Eugene Merrill states: "We should note carefully again that the whole process is by divine initiative. The Lord gives the new heart, he (re)makes them his people, and he even guarantees that they will return with all their heart. This raises the conditionality of the Mosaic covenant to the level of unconditionality." Eugene H. Merrill, *Everlasting Dominion: A Theology of the Old Testament* (Nashville: Broadman and Holman Publishers, 2006), 530.

[14] In Jeremiah 24 the sons of the *golah* or exile were equated with the good figs. According to Hugo Mantel, the "Sons of the Golah" gave priority to "personal religion" as distinct from "the cultic religion of the Temple presided over by the high priest." Hugo Mantel, "The Dichotomy of Judaism during the Second Temple," *HUCA* 44 (1973): 63.

## Position Statement

A spiritual transformation took place among the Jewish remnant in Babylon as prophesied in Jeremiah 24, such that the returnees, the *golah,* led first by Sheshbazzar and Zerubbabel and later by Ezra, understood their respective returns as prophetically motivated and as integrally related to God's larger redemptive program as described in such passages as Jeremiah 29 and 31 and Ezekiel 36 and 37.

As noted above, certain respected scholars have concluded that the Babylonian captivity did not produce lasting changes within the Jewish exile community. This conclusion has been used to support the notion that the Second Temple period that followed was at best a time of spiritual stagnation.

This study will seek to demonstrate that God used the Babylonian captivity to begin a new redemptive work among his people by establishing a spiritual or true remnant. This task will require an investigation into both Scripture and the historical record. If it can be demonstrated that Israel's exile and return marked a time of spiritual restoration rather than decline, then this era will have served as an important turning point in redemptive history with long-term significance for Israel and the nations.

This study will seek to provide evidence for the working of God's Spirit among the exiles in Babylon. Unfortunately, information relative to life in Babylon is limited. As Jill Middlemas has written, "The day-to-day life of the exiles is relatively unknown, as there is little firsthand documentation about it outside of the biblical material, which itself says little about the exilic situation."[15]

---

[15]  Jill Middlemas, *The Templeless Age* (Louisville: Westminster John Knox Press, 2007), 22.

Consequently, the Book of Ezekiel serves as an important source for understanding God's work among these exiles. In his book, *Israel in Exile,* Rainer Albertz states, "Scholars have paid little attention to the biblical picture of the exilic period."[16] One of the goals of this study will be to demonstrate just how foundational this era was to the entire Second Temple period and to the development of Second Temple Judaism.

Next, the focus of this study will turn to the early Persian period. First, the roughly two-year period recorded in the books of Haggai and Zechariah 1-8 will be examined. After that, the research will turn to a somewhat later period as recorded in the books of Ezra and Nehemiah. The investigation will seek to demonstrate that a spiritual renewal occurred among the remnant in Babylon such that both the leaders and the people understood their respective returns to Jerusalem as prophetically significant.[17]

---

[16]   Rainer Albertz, *Israel in Exile: The History and Literature of the Sixth Century B.C.E.* (Atlanta: Society of Biblical Literature, 2003), 3.

[17]   The marks of this spiritual remnant appear to include a personal recognition of sin and need of repentance, the rejection of idols, an acknowledgement of the central place of Torah in one's life, a recognition of those identified as true prophets, a commitment to fulfill one's obligation to the poor and weak members of society, and a life lived under the guidance of God's Spirit and within God's covenant. Two individuals who exemplify the remnant were Ezra the priest and Simeon (Ezra 7 and Luke 2:25-35, respectively).

## Approach to Study

As noted above, three prominent Biblical scholars have made the case that the preexilic promises were not fulfilled in the return from Babylon, and they concluded that the Second Temple era was prophetically insignificant. For example, Julius Wellhausen argued that in several key areas the return failed to live up to prophetic expectation. He argued that the postexilic period was a time of spiritual stagnation when Judaism was trapped within the framework of a legalistic religious structure. David Hubbard contrasts the preexilic condition with what he saw as the drabness of the period following the return. Recently, N. T. Wright has contended that the return was, in fact, devoid of prophetic fulfillment and concluded that the exile simply continued.

However, this negative assessment can be contrasted with the writings of scholars who hold that this era was prophetically significant. For example, J.G. McConville wrote an important article demonstrating how the books of Ezra and Nehemiah "were informed by prophecy—especially by the books of Isaiah and Jeremiah—to a far greater extent than is usually thought."[18] Additionally, in recent years a number of important discoveries

---

[18]  J.G. McConville, "Ezra-Nehemiah and the Fulfillment of Prophecy," *VT* 36, no. 2 (1986): 207. Bruce Waltke adds, "Jeremiah predicted that the captivity would last seventy years to provide the land its much needed sabbaths (cf. 2 Chron. 36:21) and to fully punish Israel for their infidelity (cf. Isa. 40:2). [In the Book of Ezra] God's eye and hand are now providentially on the second Jewish commonwealth to restore his chosen people back in the land as he had prophesied (Ezra 5:5; 7:6; 8:31)." Bruce K. Waltke, *An Old Testament Theology* (Grand Rapids: Zondervan, 2007), 796.

have been made that point to the Persian period as a time of spiritual renewal and vitality for the Jews.

Following this first chapter, the focus of the second, third, and fourth chapters will turn to the promise and fulfillment issues. The beginning point will be God's promise made in Jeremiah 24. This will serve as a foundational prophecy for this study. Other related promises that anticipate the spiritual transformation of the exiles will be considered.

It is noteworthy that these prophets, i.e. Jeremiah and Ezekiel, not only speak of the return of the exiles from Babylon, but also anticipate a more distant return that will involve greater Israel. How did these prophets foresee events unfolding as they considered Israel's future? How are these two returns related? How might the return of the *golah* foreshadow a greater return at the end of this age? The research will include relevant theological trajectories that these prophets advanced.

Another important issue that will be considered in the second chapter is that of the two remnants, i.e. the one in Jerusalem/ Judah and the other in Babylon. These two remnants existed simultaneously during the reign of King Zedekiah and experienced two very different outcomes from those which were generally anticipated by the respective groups. One method of understanding these two communities is to contrast Jeremiah's experience in Jerusalem with Ezekiel's life and ministry in Babylon. In what ways were they similar, and in what ways were they different?

Continuing to trace the sequence of events, this study will examine the impact of Jerusalem's destruction on the remnant communities. First, attention will turn to Jeremiah's experience with the group, led by Gedaliah, that stayed in Judah. How did the actions of that group align with earlier prophecy (see Jeremiah 40-44)?

Then the focus will turn to Ezekiel and to his interaction with the Jewish exiles in Babylon. Ezekiel had the unusual challenge of watching from a distant land while God's judgment fell upon Jerusalem. The exiles listened in disbelief to the reports about Jerusalem's destruction.

While exact details are missing, the text of Ezekiel hints at how news about Jerusalem's ruin was received. In what ways does the text suggest that God used the news of this disaster in a redemptive manner among the exiles in Babylon? Beyond the immediate emotion of suffering, loss, and death, how did Ezekiel understand Yahweh's ultimate plan for these Jews?

Following the analysis of the exilic period, the focus will turn to the early postexilic era. First, attention will focus on the texts of Haggai and Zechariah 1-8.[19] Then, the books of Ezra and Nehemiah will be studied. Here the issues of restoration and fulfillment of prophecy in the context of the return will be examined. How did the leaders and the returnees understand their respective returns to the land? What are the connections between earlier prophecy and fulfillment during this period of history?

Also, what can be stated concerning God's activity during this age? What is known about his plans, both near and distant, for Israel? Also, what can be stated concerning the *golah's* relationship with Yahweh? How does the relationship with God of the returnees compare with that of their preexilic forefathers? For example, are there signs that a genuine and lasting spiritual transformation occurred in Babylon?

---

[19]   This study will not include Zechariah 9-14, for while these chapters have prophetic value; their importance has limited value relative to the focus of this study.

Additionally, how did Haggai and Zechariah understand their status in relation to earlier prophecy? Paul House opened the door to this discussion when he wrote, "Prophecy was coming true in [Haggai and Zechariah's] lifetime, and the question was how much and what sorts of prophecy were being fulfilled?"[20] In this same section House adds, "Peter Ackroyd observes that Haggai and Zechariah 1-8 are especially aware that they are living in a new age marked by God's blessing. The mark of God's blessing is God's presence; the focal points of this blessing are the temple and the community of faith."[21]

The fulfillment question is central to the thesis statement of this study. Consequently, it is important to reconcile the promises of preexilic and exilic prophecy with the realities of the postexilic era. In what sense, if any, were promises being fulfilled? Also, did the postexilic prophets modify, transform, or defer to the future the fulfillment issue?

In addition, the roles that Haggai and Zechariah and also Ezra and Nehemiah played in advancing God's plan for the remnant must be considered. Commenting on Zechariah 7 and 8, House states, "Because of the remnant's responsiveness to Haggai and Zechariah the Lord will do good to Jerusalem, causing joy and gladness (8:10-19)."[22] House then adds, "Zechariah 7-8 fuses past, present, future and distant future to declare that God's jealousy for Jerusalem will result in forgiveness and blessing for the people."[23] If House is correct, then the people in Zechariah's day experienced God's forgiveness and blessing in tangible ways.

---

[20]  Paul R. House, *Old Testament Theology*, (Downers Grove: InterVarsity Press, 1998), 383.

[21]  Ibid.

[22]  Ibid., 390.

[23]  Ibid.

The fifth chapter will examine the political and archaeological data relative to the return. The return took place under the authority of the Persian monarchy. Here research will explore the political forces at work that led both to the return and also to the reestablishment of the Jewish community in Judah. The emphasis will be on the spiritual development of this community. In particular, the role that political forces played in reestablishing Jerusalem as the spiritual center for the postexilic Jewish community appears significant.

In this same chapter the archaeological evidence from this era will be examined. For example, to what extent does the archaeological record demonstrate that Judaism was marked by innovation and vitality during this time? An examination of the various changes that Judaism experienced and of the defining marks of Second Temple Judaism should aid in answering this question. Also, the role that Jerusalem played as the spiritual center for the Jewish communities in Egypt and Babylon seems particularly relevant.

The sixth chapter will draw conclusions relative to the findings of the previous chapters. Again, how convincing is the evidence suggesting that God used the Babylonian captivity to initiate a new spiritual work among this remnant? One method of evaluating this transformation will be to consider the spiritual innovations that defined the Second Temple era.

## Challenges to Understanding the Second Temple Period

As one looks at the broader picture of the Second Temple era with its struggles and failures, how can the negatives of this age be reconciled with earlier promises? For example, do not the problems described in the Book of Malachi—including defiled sacrifices (1:6-14), unfaithful priests (2:1-9), divorce and intermarriage with foreign women (2:10-16) and the withholding of tithes and sacrifices (3:6-10)—force one to conclude that the Babylonian captivity produced, at best, superficial and temporary change? These apparent incongruities deserve attention.

Turning to Haggai and Zechariah 1-8, it is noteworthy that no common consensus exists concerning the interpretation of these books. Commentators have approached these texts from a variety of viewpoints.[24] For example, Pieter Verhoef, examining the message of Haggai, says, "The three major themes of Haggai's 'theology' concern God, the temple, and the anointed one of the future."[25] Efforts to link Zerubbabel with the anointed one of the future have proved particularly challenging.

Other commentators have tried to interpret the text typologically. Verhoef agrees with Van der Woude, who says, "If the prophecy [of Haggai] is to be interpreted christologically, then the emphasis . . . is more on the second advent of Christ than on the first."[26] This appears to be an important insight.

Meyers and Meyers, pointing to the challenge exegetes face in their efforts to interpret Haggai, state, "Haggai, as it appears in the MT, was meant to be considered not only as an independent prophetic work but also as a part of the larger composite work of Haggai-Zechariah 1-8. If Haggai's present form of composition has been difficult for critics to untangle, then it is a great tribute to

---

24    See Mark J. Boda, *Haggai & Zechariah Research: A Bibliographic Survey*, (Leiden: Deo Publishing, 2003).

25    Pieter Verhoef, *The Books of Haggai and Malachi*, (Grand Rapids: Eerdmans, 1987), 32.

26    Ibid., 38.

both prophet and redactor(s) who have transmitted a polished and self-contained literary work."[27] Additionally, Meyers and Meyers note Haggai's "concern for the remnant."[28]

In a review of the recent work, *Haggai, Malachi*, by Richard Taylor and E. Ray Clendenen, the reviewer, Joseph Cathey, states, "Taylor elucidates his readers by arguing that 'temple theology' was *the* driving force behind Haggai's theology." He adds, "Taylor argues quite forcefully that the temple was the 'defining center' for much of Old Testament Judaism—religiously as well as politically."[29] This comment suggests that Taylor sees a high degree of continuity between the pre- and postexilic eras.

Roy Ciampa brings elements of the current debate regarding Haggai and Zechariah 1-8 into focus when he comments,

Of course, there was also a significant element of 'realized eschatology' in the postexilic literature. 'Haggai and Zechariah 1-8 are especially aware that they are living in a new age marked by God's blessing', but still, 'Haggai contends that full national renewal cannot take place until the temple is rebuilt.'

N.T. Wright has done the most to popularize the idea that many postexilic and Second Temple Jews believed they were still living in a state of exile, despite the fact that many of them had returned to the land. In his important

---

[27] Carol L. Meyers and Eric M. Meyers, *Haggai, Zechariah 1-8*, (New York: Doubleday and Co., 1987), lxx.

[28] Ibid., lxix.

[29] Joseph Cathey, review of *Haggai, Malachi*, by Richard Taylor and E. Ray Clendenen, *RevBL* 05 (2005): 2.

recent study, Steven M. Bryan has pointed out that 'recent scholarship on Ezra-Nehemiah has brought into focus the importance of seeing the way a partially realized eschatology is at work in the books.' In his view, 'the problem of Ezra-Nehemiah is not so much one of continuing exile but of incomplete restoration.' Furthermore, 'for the author(s) of Ezra-Nehemiah to equate the two, as Wright does, would have been to deny a key moment in the outworking of God's eschatological purposes.'[30]

Bryan's comments concerning Ezra-Nehemiah appear to hold promise for those engaged in the study of Haggai and Zechariah. His idea of "a partially realized eschatology" provides a window through which researchers can examine the early postexilic era that was so marked by the tension between fulfillment and failure.

Finally, two professors, Mark Boda[31] and Paul Redditt,[32] have made a significant contribution to the study of Haggai and Zechariah by summarizing recent research and themes, respectively. Of particular interest to Redditt and other recent commentators is the topic of redaction as it relates to determining the date and final form of Haggai and Zechariah 1-8. Other

---

[30] Roy E. Ciampa, "The History of Redemption," in *Central Themes in Biblical Theology* (Nottingham: Apollos, 2007), 284-285. In looking at the early Persian period one finds a rather "progressive restoration" in relation to Jerusalem and to the religious structures of Judaism.

[31] Mark J. Boda, "Majoring on the Minors: Recent Research on Haggai and Zechariah," *CurBR* 2 (October 2003): 33.

[32] Paul L. Redditt, "Themes in Haggai—Zechariah—Malachi," *Int* 61 (2007).

scholars explore sociological issues relevant to the return and to the early Persian period. For example, Boda states, "Drawing on literary and archaeological evidence from the Babylonian period, Barstad (1988, 1996) argues that although there was an exile, life in Judah continued along similar lines before and after the destruction of Jerusalem."[33]

Barstad's conclusions are at odds with evidence presented by the well-known archaeologist, Ephraim Stern, who argues that the archaeological evidence describes a major spiritual transformation occurring in Judah between the time of the destruction of Solomon's Temple and the reconstruction of the Second Temple.[34]

Other issues relative to the return/restoration concern Zerubbabel's role as the Davidic scion, God's return to Jerusalem, and the reunification of Israel and Judah as the people of God.[35]

In relation to Haggai's final oracle (2:20-23) Taylor sees "an eschatological promise that reaches well beyond the historical parameters of Haggai's day in terms of its fulfillment."[36] Consequently, the prophetic significance of Zerubbabel and possibly Joshua stand out as vitally important relative to the interpretation and understanding of the Book of Haggai.

---

[33] Boda, "Majoring on the Minors," 39.

[34] Ephraim Stern, "The Religious Revolution in Persian-Period Judah," in *Judah and the Judeans in the Persian Period* (Winona Lake: Eisenbrauns, 2006), 201-202.

[35] Redditt, *Haggai, Zechariah and Malachi*, 188, 191.

[36] Richard A.Taylor and E. Ray Clendenen, *Haggai, Malachi*, The New American Commentary, 21A (Nashville: Broadman and Holman, 2004), 58-59.

Historically, at the time of the Babylonian exile both Jeremiah and Ezekiel looked beyond God's judgment to Israel's restoration.[37] Jeremiah spoke of a New Covenant when God would write his law on the hearts of his people (Jer. 31:31-34). Ezekiel spoke of God cleansing Israel from her impurities and idols, of giving her a "new heart" and putting a "new spirit" in her, and of removing her "heart of stone" and giving her a "heart of flesh." God promised to accomplish this transformation through the internal working of his Spirit (Ezek. 36:25-27).

A key question to be addressed in this study is: Were these promises being fulfilled, in a demonstrable way, during the Second Temple era? This author will seek to offer textual and historical evidence that provides a positive response to this question. By implication, this conclusion assumes that in some sense the New Covenant began at that time. This study will seek to present the case that the exile and the early Persian period served as an historic hinge during which prophecy was being fulfilled with a spiritual remnant serving as the centerpiece of God's activity among the Jews of that day.

According to Ephraim Stern, a new Jewish religion developed in Babylon.[38] If so, then the full practice of this new religion

---

[37] Deuteronomy 28 and 29 speak of Israel being scattered among the nations for abandoning her covenant with Yahweh and worshiping idols. However, in chapter 30, Moses also speaks of a later time when Israel will come to her spiritual senses and return to God (vv. 1-2). When this happens, God promises to restore her fortunes and bring her back to the land (vv. 3-5). A key element in the restoration is God's promise to "circumcise your hearts and the hearts of your descendants, so that you may love him with all your heart and with all your soul, and live" (v.6).

[38] Stern, "The Religious Revolution," 203.

required that the *golah* return to the land and Jerusalem be reestablished as its spiritual center. To do this required both the rebuilding of the temple and the reestablishment of the walls and gates around Jerusalem so that the religious patterns of Judaism could be properly maintained. At that point the Jerusalem Temple could become the spiritual center for Jews in Yehud (the Persian name for Judah) and also for diaspora Jews in Babylon and Egypt.

Significantly, recent archaeological evidence points to a major religious shift taking place in Samaria during the early Persian period. This shift, a turning from polytheism to monotheism, led to the construction of the temple on Mount Gerizim. This temple was identified as "the House of YHWH."[39] In what ways, if any, did the reestablishment of Jerusalem as the spiritual center of Judaism contribute to the spiritual transformation in Samaria?


## Significance of this Study

First, this study connects in a very practical way to the study of prophecy and fulfillment. For example, if the very specific prophecy of Jeremiah 24 concerning the Jewish exiles in Babylon was not fulfilled in some demonstrable way, then other prophecies of this era must be called into question. Consequently, by implication this study impacts the field of theology proper. When God speaks a prophetic word through a prophet, can one expect to find historical evidence supporting the claim of fulfilled prophecy? Or in this case, were other factors involved that explain why the prophecy was not fulfilled?

---

[39]   Ibid., 202.

Second, this paper is designed to encourage and advance Second Temple studies. If it can be demonstrated that the Second Temple era was marked by dynamic spiritual innovation, then this period deserves further research and analysis. Additionally, the study of this era will likely open new windows of understanding in relation to the field of New Testament studies.

Finally, this work has the capacity to impact the study of pneumatology. If God's Spirit began a new work among the Jewish remnant community in Babylon, then what happened there can be understood as part of the Spirit's ongoing activity that includes Pentecost (see Acts 2), a work that foreshadows a still greater revival predicted to come at the end of this current age (Jer. 31:31-34). A proposed chiastic summary of God's historic activity in regards to Israel and Judah coming from the texts of Jeremiah and Ezekiel is:

A. David shepherds all of Israel
    B. The kingdom splits into Israel and Judah
        C. Israel goes into captivity
            D. Judah is taken to Babylon
                E. The Babylonian Exile and the New Covenant
                    begins
            D'. A remnant returns from Babylon
        C'. Greater Israel returns from captivity (Jer. 30:3)
    B'. The two kingdoms are formally reunited
      (Ezek. 37:15-22)
A'. Messianic David shepherds all of Israel (Ezek. 37:24-25)

# Chapter 2

# Israel's Spiritual Transformation as Prophesied in Jeremiah and Ezekiel

This chapter will explore the prophetic texts of Jeremiah and Ezekiel, specifically in relation to the future spiritual transformation envisioned by these prophets. Both prophets anticipated a transformation occurring, first, among the remnant taken to Babylon, and ultimately, within greater Israel. What did these two prophets foresee as they spoke about Israel's future?

## Setting the Stage

Jeremiah and Ezekiel both attest to Judah being in a state of extreme spiritual decline and in desperate need of restoration. Ezekiel explained that the root of Israel's spiritual problem went back to her time in Egypt (see Ezekiel 20). Further, these prophets exposed the idolatry and spiritual apostasy that permeated all levels of society, resulting in illegitimate worship and widespread social and ethical violations. In the words of Risa Kohn, "The disaster of 587 BCE was Yahweh's just punishment for the absolute corruption of Ezekiel's generation."[40] Radical reform was needed.

At this point, it is important to consider whether the prophecies of Jeremiah and Ezekiel, in fact, belong together. Didn't Jeremiah speak to an earlier generation than that to which Ezekiel spoke? This issue is addressed in an article written by Henry Ellison. He says,

> We are apt in our thinking to link Jeremiah with the great eighth-century prophets and to separate him from Ezekiel, whom we regard as a prophet of the exile. Even though Jeremiah's best years had been lived and the bulk of his work done before Jehoiachin went into exile with Ezekiel behind him, yet in essentials, in spite of all their differences, Jeremiah and Ezekiel belong together. The former becomes fully comprehensible only when we constantly see him in the shadow of the boiling pot, ready at any moment to boil over with destruction from the North (Jer. 1:13f.). Equally Ezekiel comes into clear focus only when we realize that he is not preaching to a doomed city some eight hundred

---

40      Risa Levitt Kohn, *A New Heart and a New Soul* (Sheffield: Sheffield Academic Press, 2002), 113. In discussing God's word of warning to the people left in Jerusalem recorded in Ezek. 2:3-8, Eugene Merrill (*Everlasting Dominion*, p.540) writes, "The oracle is to be dated in 592 BC, five years into King Jehoiachin's captivity and six years before the city and temple would be destroyed (Ezek. 1:2; 24:2; 33:21). Even with disaster on the horizon, the stubbornness of the people was so ingrained that the prophet's warnings would come to naught (3:7)."

miles away but striving desperately to bring his fellow-exiles to an understanding of the reasons for the doom so soon to fall.[41]

The words of Jeremiah and Ezekiel both complement and reinforce each other's message. While undoubtedly unwelcome at first, Jeremiah's words ultimately brought hope to the exiles in Babylon.

Returning to the topic of spiritual reform, the transformation process began with the first group removed from the land. Far from everything they knew and loved, the exiles had time to reflect on their loss.[42] The Chaldean army, led by King Nebuchadnezzar, forcibly exiled segments of the Judean population to Babylon over a period of years. Nebuchadnezzar's invasions began during the reign of Jehoiakim, ca. 604 B.C. and ended only after the complete destruction of Jerusalem in 586 B.C.[43] However, in the years prior to Jerusalem's final destruction, the prophets Jeremiah and Ezekiel repeatedly spoke not only about impending disaster, but also about a future return to the land. These years were, in fact, a truly remarkable time. While these prophets spoke of a return from Babylon, a segment of the Jewish population under the leadership of King

---

[41]     Henry L. Ellison, "The Prophecy of Jeremiah," *EvQ* 31 (July-September 1959): 145.

[42]     Though Ps. 137 may have been written at a later time, it undoubtedly reflects the sentiment of the Jews exiled in Babylon. The theme of remembrance served to increase their sense of loss and despair. They had no one to blame but themselves.

[43]     The text of Jer. 52:30 suggests that a third group was taken into exile some five years after Jerusalem's destruction.

Zedekiah remained in the land and for some nine years enjoyed relative peace.

The conventional wisdom of the day believed that those left in the land were the recipients of God's special protection while those interned in Babylon lived under God's disfavor (see Ezek. 11:14-15). Adding to the confusion were the false Jewish prophets in Babylon who promised the exiles imminent repatriation (see Jer. 29:8-9). To provide an element of clarity in an extremely confused situation, God led Jeremiah to write a letter to the Jews in Babylon (Jeremiah 29).

In this letter, God counseled his people to build houses and settle down, to increase, and to pray and seek the wellbeing of the city where they lived. Bruce Waltke notes, "[Jeremiah] proclaims that Israel's theological existence is not dependent on being in the Land."[44] Their hope was ultimately in Yahweh, not in a geographical location. Also, God warned them not to listen to those prophets predicting an imminent return to the land. He said, "When seventy years are completed for Babylon, I will come to you and fulfill my gracious promise to bring you back to this place" (v. 10). This letter actually repeated an earlier prophecy spoken by Jeremiah during the reign of King Jehoiakim (Jer. 25:11).

While Jeremiah's letter contained words of hope, it was definitely not the message of hope that the exiles, including King Jehoiachin, longed to hear. In fact, it appears that many, if not most of the Jews in Babylon, continued to cling to the words of

---

44    However, in the same paragraph Waltke (*Old Testament Theology*, p.842) adds, "Nevertheless, Israel continues to see being out of the Land in the Diaspora as an abnormal existence."

the false prophets right up to the time when news of Jerusalem's destruction reached Babylon (see Ezek. 33:30-33).

The word of Jerusalem's ruin followed by the arrival of another group of exiles eliminated all vestiges of hope that the Jews in Babylon would soon return to their homes. The dream of an imminent return vanished. God did not intervene to save Jerusalem. The temple was not protected from the invasion of foreigners. Jerusalem's leaders failed in their attempt to secure foreign assistance from nations like Egypt. Ultimately, Nebuchadnezzar's army was not repulsed. All false hopes and counterfeit support were suddenly removed, and the exiles were faced with the stark realization that what Jeremiah and Ezekiel predicted had come true. In this setting, God provided the remnant in Babylon with the following words of hope:

> Yet there will be some survivors—sons and daughters who will be brought out of it. They will come to you, and when you see their conduct and their actions, you will be consoled regarding the disaster I have brought upon Jerusalem—every disaster I have brought upon it. You will be consoled when you see their conduct and their actions, for you will know that I have done nothing in it without cause, declares the Sovereign Lord (Ezek. 14:22-23).

The arrival of these captives provided solid evidence that the prophecies of Jeremiah and Ezekiel were, in fact, true. Additionally, the earlier theologies that included the inviolability of the temple and the unbroken continuance of David's line ultimately proved false.

Nevertheless, both Jeremiah and Ezekiel continued to look beyond the destruction of Jerusalem and the exile to a time of return. Their prophecies were multifaceted and included such elements as the rebuilding of the temple, God's blessing returning to his people and to the land, Israel and Judah being reunited, godly leadership restored, including a Davidic figure ruling all of Israel, and the nations actively seeking God.

While each of these elements was important in providing the larger picture of Israel's future, this study will focus on the one element of spiritual transformation. Without genuine spiritual transformation, Israel could never maintain its covenant relationship with Yahweh or fulfill God's original design for the nation (see Exod. 19:5-6). This element was essential for Israel's future. Israel's attraction to idols and to pagan worship was simply too great and ultimately led to the unraveling of the nation's spiritual life. Consequently, spiritual transformation was essential to any future plans God had for his people.

## Jeremiah's Prophecies

In the final years of the reign of King Zedekiah, Jeremiah spoke two very different messages to the Jewish remnants (i.e., the one in Judah and the other in Babylon). Jeremiah told the remnant that remained in Judah that their only hope was to surrender to King Nebuchadnezzar and to submit to his authority (27:12). If they did that, they would live. Unfortunately, most of those left in Jerusalem ignored Jeremiah's warning and experienced the judgment of God. Nevertheless, the text suggests, there were some who listened to his warnings (39:9).

To the remnant in Babylon, Jeremiah delivered another message. He counseled them to accept the exile as from Yahweh, to increase in number, to seek and to pray for the wellbeing of the city where they lived (29:4-7). Doing this would lead to blessing and ultimately to a future repatriation to the land.[45]

About Jeremiah's words J.A. Thompson writes,

> The advice given by Jeremiah was revolutionary and altogether contrary to that being given by the prophets in Babylon . . . . The people were to settle down . . . . As to their worship of Yahweh the inference is that this can continue outside their native land and in the absence of temple and sacrifices (7:1-15, 21-22). The whole proposal was provocative and calculated to produce the sort of reaction which is described in vv. 24-28.

> More revolutionary still was the advice to *seek the welfare* (*šālôm*) of the Babylonian regime, to pray for its welfare and not its downfall. Jeremiah by these words cast the people completely adrift from all those things on which they depended and which they regarded as essential for their own well-being, a nation-state, kingship, an army, national borders, and the temple. Without all these Yahweh could give the nation new perspectives and a new understanding of their calling.[46]

---

[45]  A major and immediate unanswered question for the exiles certainly concerned the maintenance of their relationship with Yahweh without a temple or sacrifice. For those Jews in exile who recognized their covenant unfaithfulness, the normal response would have been to bring a sacrifice to the temple. This, however, was not possible.

[46]  J. A. Thompson, *The Book of Jeremiah* (Grand Rapids: Wm. B. Eerdmans, 1980), 546.

These revolutionary ideas provided the framework for spiritual transformation among the exiles living in Babylon.

To help understand the two dissimilar messages of Jeremiah, one must begin with his vision in chapter 24. There, Jeremiah saw two very different baskets of figs. The first basket held good figs and represented the remnant taken to Babylon (v.5). About these figs God spoke words of hope and transformation. God said, "I will give them a heart to know me, that I am the Lord. They will be my people, and I will be their God, for they will return to me with all their heart" (v.7). This verse begins with the promise of God's activity in giving them a "heart to know me," *lb ld't,* and concludes by stating that they will "return" to God with all their heart, *yshubu.* Verse 7 includes the covenant formula that reads, "They will be my people, and I will be their God."

Referring to the first part of verse 7, Walter Brueggemann writes these remarkable words,

> Yahweh will give Israel a new heart (24:7). It is as though the narrative knows Israel can never change its inclination (cf. 13:23). The only chance of newness is due to God's radical and underived action. The gift of a new heart (see also 31:31; Eze 36:26) is done by God, because Israel cannot change its heart. Newness out of exile is wrought by God's powerful graciousness.[47]

Another commentator, F. B. Huey, Jr., provides the following insight into God's activity: "The statement further implies that the only way a person can know God is for God to give that person a

---

[47] Walter Brueggemann, *A Commentary of Jeremiah: Exile and Homecoming* (Grand Rapids: Wm. B. Eerdmans, 1998), 218.

heart (i.e., mind, will) to do so."[48] Genuine change can occur only by divine initiative.

The necessary change that Israel could not produce on its own would be provided through God's action. The human part in the change process is described in the last part of v. 7. Here God says that they will "return" to me with all their heart. The word return, *shub*, plays a key role in the Hebrew Scriptures, especially in the prophets. J.A. Thompson and Elmer Martens write, "The root *šwb* occurs in various verbal forms in the OT with relative frequency (c. 1050x), with a concentration in Jeremiah (111x) . . . . The vb. functions in a physical sense (a person makes an about turn); it also functions in a religious sense (people turn away from or to Yahweh)."[49]

Continuing, the authors highlight the key elements that are necessarily a part of repentance. They state,

> The word *šwb* is a central word for the concept of repent. The imagery is one of a person doing a turnabout. Critical in this turnabout, if it is to be repentance, is the direction toward which one turns, namely, to Yahweh, The moves in this turning process are delineated clearly in Jer. 3:22-4:2, a veritable liturgy of repentance: acknowledging God's lordship (3:22); admitting wrongdoing (3:23), including the verbal confession, "We [I] have sinned" (3:25); addressing the shame (3:25); and affirming and adhering

---

48    F.B. Huey, Jr., *Jeremiah Lamentations*, The New American Commentary (Nashville: Broadman Press, 1993), 16:221.

49    J. A. Thompson and Elmer A. Martens, "שׁוּב," in *NIDOTTE* (Grand Rapids: Zondervan, 1997), 4:56.

to new conduct (4:1-2). For a comparable prescription of the components of repentance cf. Hosea 14:1-3[2-4].[50]

A second important passage that addresses the spiritual transformation topic is found in Jeremiah's letter to the exiles in Babylon (chap. 29). After promising to bring them back to the land when the seventy years are completed (v.10), God tells them of his plans to prosper them and give them hope and a future (v.11). God assures his people that they are not forgotten. Charles Feinberg provides insight into the promise given at the end of v. 11. He says, "Jeremiah's words 'hope and a future' (v.11) are literally 'an end and a hope,' which is a hendiadys (a figure in which a complex idea is expressed in two words linked by a coordinating conjunction) and means 'a hopeful end.'"[51]

Even though their time in Babylon was not going to be brief, as envisioned by the false prophets, they could still live with hope and also experience God's favor as they waited for their ultimate return to the land. In describing this period Moshe Reiss writes,

Nebuchadnezzar exiles the leaders among the Judeans in two waves; the first after he deposes King Jehoiachin, and the second 11 years later after he defeats and captures King Zedekiah, destroys the Temple and razes Jerusalem. Jeremiah develops a theology of exile-repentance-restoration—if the Judeans repent, God will restore them to Jerusalem . . . . This [the instruction as to how they were to live in the city where they were exiled] is a new concept

---

[50]   Ibid., 57.

[51]   Charles L. Feinberg, *Jeremiah: A Commentary* (Grand Rapids: Zondervan, 1982), 207.

of exile: work, be fruitful, and God will protect you where you are. God does not need the Temple.[52]

This theology of exile suggests an attitude for believers in every age to live by and thus experience God's favor.

Jeremiah's argument continues with God anticipating the response of the exiles, saying, "Then you will call upon me and come and pray to me, and I will listen to you. You will seek me and find me when you seek me with all your heart" (vv. 12-13).

The form of the verb "call," *qr'tm*, in the Qal second person plural, points not to the individual as much as the community responding and calling out to God. God anticipated a transformation occurring among the exiled community. Louis Jonker notes, "The basic meaning of *qr'* is to draw attention to oneself by the audible use of one's voice in order to establish contact with someone else."[53] Yahweh waited for his people to call out to him.

This word from God may also have served to reinforce the truth that even though these people were living in a distant land, God was still near to them. His presence and power were not limited to a specific geographic location. Jack Lundbom rightly states, "Prayers by the people will also be possible in a foreign land, without a temple (1 Kgs 8:46-52)."[54]

---

[52] Moshe Reiss, "Jeremiah, the Suffering Prophet, and Ezekiel, the Visionary," *JBQ* 32, no.4 (2004): 234.

[53] Louis Jonker, "קרא," *NIDOTTE*, 3:971.

[54] Jack R. Lundbom, *Jeremiah 21-36*, The Anchor Bible (New York: Doubleday, 2004), 354. While Jeremiah's letter may not have been immediately well received, it provided a new framework of thinking for the Jews living in exile.

Continuing in verse 13, God uses the verbs "seek," *bqsh*, and "find," *mts'*, in a combination that echoes Deuteronomy 4:29. Chitra Chhetri provides a helpful insight:

Moreover, the two words *bqš* and *drš* are used together in synonymous parallelism in some passages. For example, in Deut 4:29 Moses speaks to Israel: "But if from there you seek (*bqš*) the Lord your God, you will find [מצא] him if you look (*drš*) for him with all your heart and with all your soul." This is an exhortation of Moses to that generation and to the generation to come as a warning against the outcome of idolatry and subsequent returning to God with remorse for his mercy and forgiveness.[55]

In the background to these verses is again the idea of repentance. God's plan for the exiles in Babylon began with their forced removal from the land. However, during the early years of exile a battle for the hearts of the people raged. On the one hand, the Jewish false prophets predicted the imminent downfall of Babylon followed by an immediate return to the land. Robert Chisholm describes the prophecies of the false prophets as "a delusion, derived from their own divination methods and visions (14:14; 23:16, 26-38; 29:8)."[56] Jeremiah, however, prophesied that the exile would last seventy years. As the years went by and the exile continued, the influence of the false prophets undoubtedly waned.

---

55    Chitra Chhetri, "בקשׁ," *NIDOTTE*, 1:721.

56    Robert B. Chisholm, Jr., "A Theology of Jeremiah and Lamentations," in *A Biblical Theology of the Old Testament*, ed. Roy B. Zuck (Chicago: Moody Press, 1991), 345.

Additionally, the Chaldean army continued to conquer its enemies. Nebuchadnezzar's power and influence throughout the world did not appear to be decreasing. These factors surely weighed on the minds of the exiles.

## Jeremiah 31

A third important text that addresses the topic of Israel's spiritual transformation is Jeremiah 31. This chapter begins with a prophetic statement that anticipates God being the God of all the "clans" of Israel. The clans were the groups of people and/or families within the larger tribes. The wording here is noteworthy in that it highlights God's interest in accomplishing this spiritual work in the very heart of the tribes. God's commitment to spiritual renewal included transforming all levels of the social structure that existed within Jewish society.

Jeremiah 31:3 describes God's commitment to Israel and the motivation that moves God himself to see the spiritual transformation fully accomplished. The verse says, "The Lord appeared to us in the past, saying: 'I have loved you with an everlasting love; I have drawn you with loving-kindness.'" It is his covenantal loving-kindness, *hsd*, which moves God to action.

In vv. 4-5 God describes a future day when Israel is living joyfully in the land. God envisions his people planting vineyards on the hills of Samaria. In that day watchmen will call out to the people of Ephraim to go up to Zion (Jerusalem) to worship God (v.6). About the watchmen Lundbom states, "These 'watchmen' (*nōsĕrîm*) are individuals stationed at high elevations, calling the villagers to begin their pilgrimage to Jerusalem."[57] The picture is of a blessed and joyful society fully engaged in its covenantal worship of Yahweh. Additionally, the past division separating Israel in the north from Judah in the south is gone. The tribes are once again united.

Continuing in the chapter, one finds in verse 8 a "great throng" returning from the north and coming back to the land. Here one observes a major reversal. In the past, invading armies came from the north and took Israel and Judah off into captivity, whereas now the people are miraculously returning from the north to the land. The miraculous nature of this return is highlighted in that the weakest of society—the blind and the lame, expectant mothers and women in labor—are all being shepherded safely back (vv.9-10). About this return, Thompson says, "Though the people come weeping (cf. Ps. 126), Yahweh will lead them, will comfort them (Isa. 40:11), and guide them by flowing streams on a *smooth (yāšār,* "straight") way where they will not stumble."[58]

The return described here in Jeremiah 31 appears to be much greater than that of Judah coming back from Babylon. This return pictures Ephraim (Israel) returning to the land. The emphasis of the chapter is on the return of all the clans of Israel, and in particular on Ephraim, the dominant tribe of the north. God gathers them from the ends of the earth.

From this, it can be concluded that Jeremiah anticipated two returns. The first return would be of Judah coming back from Babylon. A second, larger return will occur in the distant future. Because of the similarities, it appears that the first return foreshadowed the second. What are the similarities? First, both

---

57    Lundbom, *Jeremiah,* 418.
58    Thompson, *Jeremiah,* 570.

returns include similar language. For example, the language of hope for the descendants (v.17) is similar to the words of hope expressed to Judah in 29:11. Second, like Judah, Israel will return both to the land and to Yahweh (31:19). Third, both returns come from the north.

As God disciplined Judah, so he also will discipline Ephraim. Verse 18 says, "I have surely heard Ephraim's moaning: 'You disciplined me like an unruly calf, and I have been disciplined. Restore me, and I will return, because you are the Lord my God.'"

Referring to Ephraim's repentance, Thompson and Martens say,

A scenario of Ephraim's (Israel's) repenting (*šwb*) is given in Jer. 31:18-20, another passage in which the prophet engages in wordplay. The disciplined party pleads that God will restore (*šwb*) him so that he may return (*šwb*). Following the straying (*šwb*), states Ephraim, he repented (*nḥm*) (31:19).

The personal relationship of God and people is underscored by the use of *nḥm*, a synonym of *šwb*.[59]

Israel's history was marked by turning. Unfortunately, the turning had most often been away from Yahweh. Here, however, the turning will be back to Yahweh, followed by restoration. Another important element connected to Israel's return and spiritual transformation will be the establishment of "a new covenant with the house of Israel and with the house of Judah" (v.31). This new covenant is described in the comments that follow.

---

[59]   Thompson and Martens, 57.

Writing on this passage, Femi Adeyemi states,

The New Covenant in Jeremiah 31:31-34 has been regarded by some biblical scholars as the highest point of the Old Testament Scriptures. This is because it promises (a) genuine spirituality ("I will put My law within them and on their heart I will write it"), (b) intimate fellowship between Israel and Yahweh ("I will be their God, and they shall be My people"), (c) universal knowledge of God on the part of Israel ("they will all know Me"), and (d) absolute forgiveness of sin ("I will forgive their iniquity").[60]

An important difference between the two covenants is that the Old Covenant was written on stone and existed externally to Israel, while the New Covenant exists within the hearts of God's people. God says that he will put his "law in their minds and write it on their hearts." The focal point of the newness of the covenant is not on its content but rather on the fact that this New Covenant will reside in their hearts. The New Covenant is designed to establish a true and lasting relationship between God and his people.

Does the text anticipate when this New Covenant will be established? Has it already occurred? Both of the time markers in vv. 1 and 31, "at that time" and "the time is coming," respectively, and the fact that both Israel and Judah are united and living back in the land, point to a still future fulfillment. Again Adeyemi writes,

---

[60]  Femi Adeyemi, "What Is the New Covenant 'Law' in Jeremiah 31:33?" *BSac* 163 (July-September 2006): 312.

The context of Jeremiah 31 shows that these "days" refer to the yet-future restoration of Israel to her land, when the Messiah returns. Israel will be gathered from "the remote parts of the earth" (v. 8), and God will "keep him [Israel] as a shepherd keeps his flock" (v. 10). The nation will be filled with joy (vv. 11-14), her fortunes will be restored (v. 23), and she will be blessed by the Lord (v. 23).[61]

The questions of where and when this promise will be fulfilled are particularly relevant to this study. First, where will this be fulfilled? All the textual markers point to an earthly fulfillment. For example, the text speaks of the "hills of Samaria," the "hills of Ephraim," and going "up to Zion" (vv. 5-6). Second, when will all this take place? Adeyemi concludes, "The New Covenant law will be in force in the future millennial age, guiding pardoned Israelites who have been redeemed from the bondage of sin that had caused them to be scattered (23:1-8), just as the Mosaic Law guided the nation after they were redeemed from bondage in the land of Egypt."[62] This question of fulfillment will be revisited and examined in more detail later.

## Jeremiah 32

Jeremiah 32 speaks about the time when, during the siege of Jerusalem, God commanded Jeremiah to purchase a field in Anathoth. After completing the purchase and sealing the deed, Jeremiah prays to God, requesting insight into God's plans. God

---

61  Ibid., 317.

62  Ibid., 321.

responds to Jeremiah's prayer. In his response God explains that he was handing Jerusalem over to the Babylonians because of sins committed by both Israel and Judah. All levels of society had become corrupt (v.32). In addition, God says, "They set up their abominable idols in the house that bears my Name and defiled it. They built high places for Baal in the Valley of Ben Hinnom to sacrifice their sons and daughters to Molech, though I never commanded, nor did it enter my mind, that they should do such a detestable thing and so make Judah sin" (vv.34-35).

God then shifts his focus and looks past the impending destruction of Jerusalem to the time when he will regather his people (v.37). Further, he expresses his covenant commitment to Israel (v.38). Finally, he describes the internal, spiritual work that he will perform in the hearts of his people so that they will maintain their covenantal relationship with him. He says,

> I will give them singleness of heart and action, so that they will always fear me for their own good and the good of their children after them. I will make an everlasting covenant with them: I will never stop doing good to them, and I will inspire them to fear me, so that they will never turn away from me. I will rejoice in doing them good and will assuredly plant them in this land with all my heart and soul (vv.39-41).

The setting, the context, and all the descriptions in the first part of chapter 32 depict the impending Babylonian destruction. However, beginning in v.37 the text shifts and looks forward to Judah returning to the land. Broadly, this chapter describes Judah's imminent destruction, and then anticipates Judah's return from Babylon. The return speaks of the "the territory of

Benjamin," "the villages around Jerusalem," "the towns of Judah" and "the towns of the hill country," and also "the western foothills and of the Negev" (v.44). Clearly, the focus of this chapter centers on the Babylonian captivity along with the promised return.

In his discussion of this chapter Ronald Clements writes,

> The content of the message of hope is clear, that there will one day be a return to normal life and business and all the processes of work and agriculture in the land that was at that time so ravaged and threatened by the armies of Babylon. The ominous and fearful setting, made all the more poignant by the fact of Jeremiah's own personal imprisonment at the hands of his own people, makes a great contrast to the simplicity and certainty of God's word of hope. At a time when Jeremiah could feel the cold grip of near despair and hopelessness he found that the word of God alone provided a new assurance for the future. Nor at this stage is there any indication as to how soon the return to normality would come about, nor even in what specific political context it would be realized. It is simply a clear and firm assurance that the word of God alone is the ultimate ground and certainty of hope.

> The sealing of the deed is then made the subject of a beautiful and moving prayer from Jeremiah (32:16-25) in which the prophet reflects upon the nature of God and on the way in which this merciful and saving nature has been revealed in the history of the sinful and undeserving people of Israel.[63]

---

[63] Ronald E. Clements, "Jeremiah, Prophet of Hope," *RevExp* 78 (summer 1981): 351.

The contrasts in chapter 32 could hardly be greater. On the one hand, God is about to hand the city of Jerusalem over to the Babylonians (v.28). They will burn the city down (v.29). God's wrath will be poured out on that generation. Yet, in the future, God will bring his people back and let them live in safety (v.37b). He will make an everlasting covenant with them, he will "never stop doing good to them" (v.40a). God will inspire his people to fear him, and he will rejoice in "doing them good" (vv.40b-41).

God's commitment to Israel's spiritual transformation is unwavering. As he explains in verse 39, he promises to give them "singleness of heart and action," *lb 'hd vdrk*. Singleness, *'hd*, is used here as an adjective which Philip Jensen defines as "single, unique, singular, a certain, each." Israel's heart will no longer be divided. To this Jensen adds, "The prophets realized that only God could ultimately grant (lit.) 'one heart and one way,' a single-minded devotion to God and a common lifestyle to his will (Jer. 32:39; Ezek. 11:19)."[64] As has been emphasized above, this spiritual transformation will be accomplished uniquely through God's sovereign power.

## Jeremiah 50

The final passage to be examined in Jeremiah that addresses the issue of spiritual transformation is found in chapter 50. Verses 4-5 say,

> In those days, at that time, declares the Lord, the people of Israel and the people of Judah together will go in tears to seek the Lord their God. They will ask the way to Zion

---

[64]    Philip P. Jenson, "אחד," *NIDOTTE*, 1:349-350.

and turn their faces toward it. They will come and bind themselves to the Lord in an everlasting covenant that will not be forgotten.

This passage is strikingly similar to the New Covenant promise of Jeremiah 31. It combines greater Israel and Judah in an anticipated return that includes the future time markers, "in those days" and "at that time." Consequently, this New Covenant promise awaits a still future fulfillment.

The description of this return, like the account given in chapter 31 includes the element of tears. The root word, *bkh*, is defined by John Oswalt as "to weep, cry, shed tears." He adds, "In Hebrew it means 'to weep by reason of joy or sorrow, the latter including lament, complaint, remorse or repentance.'"[65]

Oswalt also notes that the root is used in five different ways, including the crying associated with joy, the crying of distress, the specific form of distress associated with death, weeping associated with pleading or complaint, and a final weeping associated with repentance.[66] He says,

The final usage of "weeping" is unique to the OT. It is the weeping of repentance. In other cultures of the ancient near east weeping out of remorse or sorrow for punishment is known, but never sheer sorrow over having offended the deity. Both of these occur in the OT. An example of the former would be found in Jud 21:2 where the Israelites weep because of their folly in decimating Benjamin. On the other hand is the weeping of Josiah at the reading of

---

[65]    John N. Oswalt, "בכה," *TWOT*, 1:107.

[66]    Ibid., 108.

the Law (II Kgs 22:19), or the weeping of Israel when she returns to her God (Jer. 31:9; 50:4).[67]

In summary, what did Jeremiah understand about Judah and Israel's future in those final days of the reign of King Zedekiah? First, he understood that God was giving the city of Jerusalem over to Nebuchadnezzar and to his army. The city would be destroyed. Second, he knew that God had stated that the exile in Babylon would last seventy years (25:11; 29:10). Third, Jeremiah knew that at the end of the seventy years God would judge Babylon and bring his people back to the land (25:12-14; 29:10). Fourth, Jeremiah anticipated a day when greater Israel would return to the land. This return would be accompanied by a New Covenant that would include spiritual transformation, forgiveness of sin, abundant prosperity and peace, and a new Davidic ruler (31:31-34; 33:14-26).

All of this information, including Judah's imminent destruction, appears to have overwhelmed Jeremiah. Trying to imagine how God would restore everything that was so broken left Jeremiah utterly perplexed. He began his prayer in chapter 32 recognizing God as the Creator of all things, and then makes this simple but profound statement to God: "Nothing is too hard for you" (v.17).

## Ezekiel's Prophecies

As a priest as well as a prophet, Ezekiel had a special concern for the spiritual condition of the Jews living in exile. However, ministry for him proved doubly difficult in that he worked in

---

[67]    Ibid.

a setting filled with spiritual counterfeits, i.e. false prophets. These spiritual charlatans served as an ongoing threat, not only to Ezekiel, but also to the exiles, who were enticed by the prophetic utterances of these prophets.

An additional factor that impacted Ezekiel's ministry is noted by the commentator Yehezkel Kaufmann:

The cloud of Manasseh's age hovers over the book of Ezekiel. The vision of temple abominations in chapters 8-10, the historical surveys of chapters 16, 20, and 23 paint the whole of Israelite history in the lurid colors of the age of Manasseh, indicating how far the memory of that age threw a pall over all that came after."[68]

To counter the residual negative and pervasive influence of Manasseh's age, God's Spirit intervened both actively and visibly in Ezekiel's life and ministry. Beginning in chapter 1, Ezekiel saw a vision of God's glory. He responded by falling on his face (1:28). Next, Ezekiel heard God's voice speaking to him, commanding him to stand on his feet. The text says, "As he spoke, the Spirit came into me and raised me to my feet, and I heard him speaking to me" (2:2). Daniel Block has noted, "Ezekiel may well be described as the most 'spiritual' prophet of the OT. Indeed he may well be designated 'the prophet of the spirit,' and that for more than one reason."[69] From the outset, Ezekiel's ministry was marked by a powerful moving of God's Spirit.

---

[68] Yehezkel Kaufmann, *The Religion of Israel*, trans. Moshe Greenberg (Chicago: The University of Chicago Press, 1960), 435.

[69] Daniel I. Block, "The Prophet of the Spirit: the Use of *RWH* in the Book of Ezekiel," *JETS* 32 (March 1989): 28.

Following these experiences, Ezekiel ministered to the exiles. Additionally, Ezekiel prophesied against the "high places" left in Judah that served as centers for pagan worship. God promised that these pagan altars would be smashed and the worshipers killed. However, God added,

> But I will spare some, for some of you will escape the sword when you are scattered among the lands and nations. Then in the nations where they have been carried captive, those who escape will remember me—how I have been grieved by their adulterous hearts, which have turned away from me, and by their eyes, which have lusted after their idols. They will loathe themselves for the evil they have done and for all their detestable practices (Ezek. 6:8-9).

This passage pictures a remnant of Judean Jews surviving the coming judgment and being taken into captivity. Out of the land and living in exile, they will recognize their sin against Yahweh and repent. Like Jeremiah, Ezekiel anticipated a day of repentance and Israel's return to Yahweh.

God's judgment upon the remnant left in Jerusalem proved severe. For example, in chapter 11 God's Spirit took Ezekiel to Jerusalem, where he witnessed the pagan practices of Judah's spiritual leaders. These leaders wrongly believed that they were somehow safe from God's judgment. However, as Ezekiel prophesied, the leader, Pelatiah, fell dead (v.13a). Startled, Ezekiel fell facedown, fearing that God was about to destroy the entire remnant of Jews in Jerusalem (v.13b).

God did not destroy that remnant, but instead intervened to transform Ezekiel's thinking. He explained to Ezekiel that his attention was focused on the exiles in Babylon. About them he said, "Although I sent them far away among the nations and scattered them among the countries, yet for a little while I have been a sanctuary for them in the countries where they have gone" (v.16). This is a foundational passage for understanding God's work among the exiles.

Richard Averbeck defines the word "sanctuary," *mqdsh*, as "the place where the Israelites worshiped the Lord and offered their various kinds of offerings and sacrifices to the Lord under the supervision of the priest."[70] This word is derived from the Hebrew root, *qdsh*, a word used to distinguish between that which is sacred or holy and the profane. The word "sanctuary" in this passage cannot be understood as a building. As Averbeck states, "As in English, where the word 'sanctuary' can sometimes refer to a refuge, there are two instances where the Lord refers to himself metaphorically as the sanctuary (i.e., refuge) of faithful Israelites in distress (Isa. 8:14; Ezek. 11:16)."[71] God acted as a refuge for his exiled people. He provided for their safety and care. He was their sanctuary.

Then in verse 18 of chapter 11, God anticipates the return of the exiles to the land, saying, "They will return to it and remove all its vile images and detestable idols." Was this prophecy historically fulfilled? This will be an important topic in the next chapters.

Continuing, the text says, "I will give them an undivided heart and put a new spirit in them; I will remove from them their heart of stone and give them a heart of flesh. Then they will follow my decrees and be careful to keep my laws. They will be my people, and I will be their God" (vv.19-20). The promise here is strikingly similar to that given through Jeremiah (Jer. 32:39-40).

---

[70]    Richard E. Averbeck, "מִקְדָּשׁ," *NIDOTTE*, 2:1079.

[71]    Ibid., 1080.

By contrast, the verse that follows speaks of God's judgment on those who continue in idolatry: "But as for those whose hearts are devoted to their vile images and detestable idols, I will bring down on their own heads what they have done, declares the Sovereign Lord" (v.21).

Verses 19-20 are critically important for understanding the spiritual transformation that Ezekiel anticipated taking place among the exiles. Noting the similarity of these two verses with chapter 36:26-27, Peter Craigie writes,

> Thus while some scholars may be correct in their view that several of the verses now being considered represent insertions in the text from a later period in Ezekiel's ministry (note particularly the similarity between verses 19-20 and Chapter 36:26-27), nevertheless the general substance of this passage must be integral to the prophet's great vision of Jerusalem. Only then does the vision as a whole really make sense as a part of Ezekiel's prophetic ministry to the exiles.[72]

Craigie also highlights the significance of this chapter to the transforming work that was occurring in the thinking of these exiles. He says,

> Thinking themselves [as exiles] to be useless, they had looked to others in far off Jerusalem to provide a source of hope. But the tables were turned. If there was hope to be found, it lay *within them*, not in the empty hands of others

---

[72] Peter C. Craigie, *Ezekiel* (Philadelphia: The Westminster Press, 1983), 77.

far away. The citizens of Jerusalem had already written off the exiles as irrelevant to the future of their city. Indeed, the exiles themselves thought that there was nothing they could do. But now they were learning that the weak of this world were the ones through whom God would work. And such new hope was not without its attendant anxiety, for it involved awesome responsibility (italics added).[73]

Clearly the exiles in Babylon found themselves in a weak and dependent condition in relation to the Babylonian empire and, in particular, in relation to their hopes of repatriation. Their hope was uniquely in Yahweh and in him alone.

Significantly, God promised to give them an "undivided heart," *lb 'hd*. This corresponds with the promise in Jeremiah 32:39, which the NIV translates as "singleness of heart" (see comment in the Jeremiah section). Further, God promises a "new spirit," *hdshh ruh*, Pieter Verhoef writes,

As part of the promised return of Israel (Ezek. 11:16-25), God will give them an undivided heart (lit. "one heart") and will put in them a "new spirit" (v. 19). The initiative is clearly God's. He will "give" (*ntn*) it to them, lest they should claim to themselves the praise given them in v. 18. It will be a free gift of his Spirit.[74]

Chapter 11 of Ezekiel is filled with profound spiritual insight and promise. In this chapter, God stresses that prior to their return, fundamental change had to take place in the hearts of his

---

[73]   Ibid., 79.

[74]   Pieter A. Verhoef, "חדשׁ," *NIDOTTE*, 2:35.

people. A radical transformation of the human spirit was needed. However well-intentioned or committed to change these Jewish exiles may have felt, in themselves they did not have the ability to change! Divine intervention was essential.

In combination with giving them an undivided heart and putting a new spirit in them, God promises to "remove from them their heart of stone and give them a heart of flesh." Daniel Block elaborates on this promise when he says,

> Ezekiel expands on Jeremiah's words further by describing the renewal in terms of a heart transplant. The expression "stony heart" (*lēb hā'eben*) concretizes the disposition of the Israelites, previously described as "hard-hearted" (*ḥizqê lēb*, 2:4) and "stubborn-hearted" (*qěšê lēb*, 3:7). The only solution for people like this is radical surgery, the removal of the defective and fossilized organ and its replacement with a sensitive and responsive heart, "a heart of flesh" (*lēb bāśār*).[75]

But when might this promise be fulfilled? The textual evidence from both Jeremiah and Ezekiel points to a transformation occurring prior to repatriation. God promised to purge this remnant of those who revolted and rebelled against him. Rebels would not return to the land (Jer. 29:20-32; Ezek. 20:38). Also, Deuteronomy 30 promised a regathering after the people turned back to Yahweh (vv. 2-5).

In Ezekiel 11:16-25, God describes his work among the exiles in Babylon. Some of them will be judged (11:21). Others

---

[75]   Daniel I. Block, *The Book of Ezekiel: Chapters 1-24* (Grand Rapids: Eerdmans, 1997), 353.

will repent and experience a major heart transformation. This will take place prior to the return to what Block describes as "a polluted land—defiled by centuries of detestable (*šiqqûṣîm*) and abominable (*tôʿăbôt*) conduct, not by pagans but by Israelites themselves. Whereas Yahweh promised to deliver his people himself, responsibility for ridding the land of its contaminants was left with the people."[76]

As Block notes, "God promised to transform his people prior to returning them to the land. However, the responsibility of ridding the land of its spiritual pollutants would rest in the hands of the *golah* (11:18)."[77] This is a prophetically important aspect of the return.

This section (chapters 8-11) closes with the vision taken up from Ezekiel, followed by Ezekiel addressing the exiles. Significantly, this passage does not contain the common distant future markers, such as "in that day" or "at that time." Consequently, this passage applies directly to the exiles in Babylon and to their children. They would be the ones who would return and cleanse the land of idols.

# Ezekiel 14

Turning next to chapter 14, one finds a group of the elders coming to Ezekiel seeking a word from God. However, due to the idolatrous condition of their hearts and the insincerity of their words, God rejects their request. They presumed to inquire of Yahweh using methods typical of their pagan neighbors. It seems

---

[76]    Ibid., 352.

[77]    Ibid.

that they had been so seduced by pagan thinking and practices that they no longer recognized the uniqueness of Yahweh. To their surprise, Yahweh refuses their request!

As John Bright states, "The ancient paganisms were all polytheistic, with dozens of gods arranged in complex pantheons. These gods were for the most part personifications of the forces of nature or other cosmic functions, and without any particular moral character."[78] The Jews of this period had apparently developed their own pantheon with Yahweh holding a place of prominence within the system.

It is known that over the centuries the Jews living in Israel had incorporated a number of pagan practices into their belief system, including the worship of the Asherahs (female deities; see 2 Chron. 33:19). For example, they had come to believe that at certain high places, or trees, or steles a person could have direct access to the spiritual realm. In an archaeological study west of Hebron and southeast of Lachish researchers found evidence supporting the theory that "*l'ashérah* des textes bibliques semble bien désigner l'arbre sacré lié au culte traditionnel de l'ancien Israël, situé à côté de l'autel et de la stele (*maṣṣēbāh*)" [The Asherah of the biblical texts seems to refer to a sacred tree tied to traditional worship in ancient Israel, located next to the altar and the stele].[79] From this statement, one can conclude that to the untrained observer it would have been virtually impossible to distinguish between the religious rites practiced in preexilic Judah and those practiced by their pagan neighbors.

---

[78]  John Bright, "Faith and Destiny," *Int* 5, no. 1 (1951): 6.

[79]  André Lemaire, "Les Inscriptions de Khirbet El-Qôm et L'Ashérah de YHWH," *RB* 84 (1977): 607.

Yahweh would no longer tolerate the religious syncretism that existed in preexilic Judah. John Bright notes, "[Yahweh] is no personification of natural force to be appeased by ritual; he is a personal Being who acts in nature and history, and whose moral will is simply to be obeyed."[80] Unfortunately, these exiled Jews held on to their pagan methods as they approached Yahweh. Change required time, patience, and, in this case, direct divine intervention to transform the thinking of these people (Ezek. 14:4-5).

God, in fact, turned the tables on these elders (14:4b). As Block states, "They are the ones who must answer to him; not he to them. He is Yahweh! The covenant Lord has been affronted first by their apostasy, and now by their insincerity. All he can see is the multitudes of idols on their minds; Yahweh's response bypasses their concerns altogether."[81]

The words that follow (v.5) summarize God's plan of action in confronting their idolatrous condition. The text says, "I will do this to *recapture* the hearts of the people of Israel, who have all deserted me for their idols" (italics added). The word "recapture," *tpsh* is defined by A.H. Konkel as "take hold of, capture, occupy."[82] He notes that "the vb. is commonly used in relation to war."[83]

Daniel Block expands on this unusual expression:

The verb *tāpaś* is applied elsewhere to the forceful apprehension of prisoners and captives. The full expression *tāpaś bĕlibbām*, "to seize by their hearts," treats the people's

---

[80]   Bright, "Faith and Destiny," 6.

[81]   Block, *Ezekiel*, 427.

[82]   A.H. Konkel, "תפש," *NIDOTTE*, 4:326.

[83]   Ibid.

"thoughts" as concrete extensions of their persons. But this odd expression highlights the locus of their problem. There is no point in dealing with externals, when the disposition of their hearts needs to be arrested.[84]

Lamar Cooper provides additional insight into this verse with these words:

An alternative to the NIV interpretation is that of Greenberg: even though Israel's sin was presently only in their heart, that is, "idolmindedness," God was able to catch them "at their thoughts" (cf. Num 5:13). Both ideas are in the passage, and either fits the context (cf. v. 11). In the midst of such an idolatrous culture, a battle for the minds of Israel was being fought.[85]

The battle for the minds of the exiles was being waged by God and his prophet in Babylon; God's unambiguous call in v.6 was "Repent! Turn from your idols and renounce all your detestable practices!" The text reads, *shubu vhshibu.* The command is formed by a Qal imperative followed by the "active" Hiphil imperative. The Hiphil form of *shub* is used some 350 times in the OT and is defined as "bring back, lead back, transport, restore."[86] A strong admonition!

---

84   Block, *Ezekiel,* 427.

85   Lamar Eugene Cooper, Sr., *Ezekiel,* The New American Commentary, 17 (Nashville: Broadman and Holman Publishers, 1994), 160.

86   Thompson and Martens, 55. It appears that here the hiphil carries the reflexive sense of "turn yourselves away from your idols," that is most commonly found in the niphil form of the verb.

If the elders came seeking a word of hope in relation to Jerusalem's fate, they did not receive it. God's decision to judge Zedekiah, the remnant in Jerusalem, and the city itself would not be reversed. As Daniel Block notes,

> Ezekiel is not hereby interceding on Israel's behalf to stay God's hand; his call for repentance holds out no hope that Jerusalem will be saved. On the other hand, it does reflect Yahweh's deepest desire: the willing obedience of his people (cf. v. 11), and in so doing it opens the door just a crack to a new future for the immediate audience.[87]

In this text God makes a forceful appeal to the will of these exiles. Importantly, his call to them leaves the final decision in their hands. He will not be accused of having coerced them into repentance.

In the verses that follow (vv. 7-8), God enlarges on his plan for dealing with those who defect from him and serve idols. Blinded by their idolatry, these elders presume to come and inquire of God through the intermediary of Ezekiel. Apostasy marked by double-mindedness will not be tolerated by Yahweh.

In v.8 God says that three things will happen to anyone choosing to follow the path of apostasy. First, God says that he will "set [his] face against that man."[88] Second, he states, "[I will] make him an example and a byword." Third and most

---

[87] Block, *Ezekiel*, 428.

[88] Daniel Block points out that for God to set his face against a person is the antithesis of setting his face on or looking with favor upon someone. In fact, the phrase "to set the face upon," referring to God, is not found in the entire Book of Ezekiel. Ibid., 430.

ominously God adds, "I will cut him off from my people." As Block says,

> The prospects for the people who have approached Ezekiel for a word from God are frightening. Not only has the bond between them and the land been severed; now they are threatened with an ultimate and final break with their God . . . . Still, the previous call for repentance has left the door open to a better fate. The doom of those who remain in Jerusalem is sealed, but if the exiles turn their faces toward Yahweh alone, and abandon their own forms of idolatry, they may escape his fury. They still have the choice-they may acknowledge Yahweh on his terms voluntarily now, or be forced to do so involuntarily on that great and terrible day.[89]

Biblical history appears to have reached a crisis point. Israel's future depends on the response of this remnant in Babylon! It would be hard to overstate the significance of what transpired there. The lines between divine sovereignty and human responsibility appear blurred.

Next, God's attention turns to the false prophets who lived among the exiles in Babylon. Yahweh spoke a special word of judgment against them. Again Block says,

> The exilic community was apparently plagued by prophets who capitalized on the insecurity of the people by offering reassuring (counterfeit) oracles. But the professional prophet who caters to idolaters and issues pronouncements

---

[89]    Ibid., 431.

as if they had come from Yahweh becomes an accomplice in their crime (cf. Deut. 13:2-6 [Eng. 1-5]; 18-20).[90]

God's intervention was both measured and focused. His purpose was to cleanse the community in exile of those who were unrepentant in their idolatry and of the lying prophets. Yahweh summarizes his plan and what will be accomplished by his actions in v.11: "Then the people of Israel will no longer stray from me, nor will they defile themselves any more with all their sins. They will be my people, and I will be their God."

Turning next to another topic of both historic and prophetic importance, Ezekiel, like Jeremiah, addresses the topic of covenant. The term covenant, *brit*, occurs six times in chapter 16. Ezekiel, like Jeremiah, states the indisputable fact that Israel had broken its covenant with Yahweh (16:59). God's solution, however, was not to abandon Israel, but to reestablish his covenant with her. As noted in the previous section, Jeremiah spoke of God establishing a New Covenant with Israel. Ezekiel describes this future covenant in a slightly different manner, calling it an "everlasting covenant," *brit 'olm*

To better understand these prophetic voices, one must begin by examining the significance of covenant, *brit*, in ancient Israel. Elmer Smick writes, "The covenant concept in the OT presents a very rich and complex tradition and that the covenant is not primarily legalistic or moralistic but cultic, that is, tied to religious practice."[91] The covenant was maintained primarily through

---

90    Ibid., 431-2. Herein lies a special word of warning for religious leaders today who would cater to the unbelief and spiritual rebellion of the culture to the exclusion of God's expressed will!

91    Elmer B. Smick, "ברית," *TWOT*, 1:129.

agreed upon religious practices. These practices were designed to maintain and also restore Israel's relationship with Yahweh. Repentance was an essential element in the restoration process.

Unfortunately, due to Israel's inclination to apostasy and her unwillingness to repent, she was drawn to the less costly and sensually pleasing practices of her neighbors. However, these practices led not to freedom, but to bondage. Consequently, some new element was needed. For the covenant to succeed, a fundamental change was necessary, not because the covenant was flawed, but because Israel was flawed.

Israel's history demonstrated that without some concrete and lasting change within the heart of the nation, God's covenant with her could not achieve its goal. Genuine spiritual transformation was needed. God must intervene. Both Jeremiah and Ezekiel predicted that God would, in fact, act.

The result would be what Ezekiel referred to as an "everlasting covenant." This covenant was to be established with a transformed people who would return to the land and live in covenant obedience with Yahweh. Under these conditions, Ezekiel spoke of God's blessing returning and God again placing his sanctuary in Israel (Ezek. 37:26).

Israel needed to experience what Daniel Block describes as the "radical spiritual revitalization of the nation."[92] Nothing less would do. This revitalization is described in Ezekiel 36. After promising to take them out of the nations and bring them back to the land, God says,

> I will sprinkle clean water on you, and you will be clean; I
> will cleanse you from all your impurities and from all your

---

[92]   Block, "The Prophet of the Spirit," 39.

idols. I will give you a new heart and put a new spirit in you; I will remove from you your heart of stone and give you a heart of flesh. And I will put my Spirit in you and move you to follow my decrees and be careful to keep my laws (vv. 25-27).

God here promises to bring about a threefold renewal of his people. First, God promises to "sprinkle," *zrq*, them with clean water. Charles Feinberg identifies this phrase as "an allusion to the Mosaic rites of purification (see Num. 19:17-19; Isa. 4:4; Zech. 13:1; Ps. 119.9)."[93] About this word, "sprinkle," Victor Hamilton states,

Although used most often with the sprinkling or throwing of blood, it is used 3x to refer to the sprinkling of water (Num. 19:13, 20; Ezek. 36:25). The two references in Num 19 are to purification from impurity resulting from contact with or proximity to something dead. It is such procedures that more than likely inspired Ezekiel to speak of God's forthcoming purification of Israel as a sprinkling of pure water on them. In fact, the Targum makes the connection clear, "And I will remit your sins like those that are cleaned with the water of sprinkling and with the ashes of the heifer of the guilt offering."[94]

---

93 Charles L. Feinberg, *The Prophecy of Ezekiel: The Glory of the Lord* (Chicago: Moody Press, 1969), 209.

94 Victor P. Hamilton, "זרק," *NIDOTTE*, 1:1153-4.

Block provides an additional insight:

The description [of the cleansing] mixes the metaphors of priestly cleansing rituals and blood sprinkling ceremonies . . . . In the present context, the issue is not simply an external ceremonial cleansing accompanying the internal renewal described in vv. 26-27, but a wholesale cleansing from sin performed by Yahweh, a necessary precondition to normalizing the spiritual relationship between Yahweh and his people.[95]

Second, to underscore just how problematic Israel's spiritual condition had become, God promises to perform a heart transplant within his people. Verse 26 virtually repeats the words of 11:19. This verse, in particular, provides a window into the larger human condition. As Block notes,

*Lēb* and *rûaḥ* represent the person's internal locus of emotion, will, and thought . . . . Ezekiel recognized the problem of rebellion and sin against Yahweh to be more deeply ingrained than mere external acts. Ezekiel concretizes the metaphor by describing the heart as *stone*, which speaks of coldness, insensitivity, incorrigibility, and even lifelessness (cf. 1 Sam. 25:37). Ezekiel knew whereof he spoke, having had to deal with the obduracy of his people from the time of his call. But God has been struggling with the problem for centuries. The present solution is more radical even than the circumcision of the

---

[95] Daniel I. Block, *Ezekiel: Chapters 25-48* (Grand Rapids: Eerdmans, 1998), 354-355.

heart prescribed by Deut. 30:6-8. The only answer is the removal of the petrified organ and its replacement with a warm, sensitive, and responsive heart of flesh (*bāśār*).[96]

The contrast between stone and flesh deserves some reflection because of the manner in which flesh is so often used in the Bible. This term, *bshr*, often points to man's mortal and weak nature (Isa. 40:6; Jer. 17:5), to sinful humankind in general (Gen. 6:13, 17), or even all humanity (Joel 2:28). Here, however, as Robert Chisholm demonstrates,

> [The] heart is viewed as the seat of one's moral life and volition, stone symbolizes spiritual insensitivity, and flesh signifies spiritual receptivity. The Lord himself will supernaturally and sovereignly effect this transformation . . . in conjunction with exiled Israel's spiritual cleansing and return to the land.[97]

What is truly remarkable here is the construction of the verse that follows (v. 27). The text reads, *v't ruhi 'tn bqrbkm*, "my Spirit I will place in you" [author's translation]. The new spirit will be enlivened by God's Spirit. This leads to the third element of revitalization where God promises that the end result of his work among his people will be that they actively live in conformity to his will.

God says to Israel, "[I will] move you to follow my decrees and be careful to keep my laws" (v. 27b). With God as the subject, the word "move," *'shh*, reflects the divine will actively at work shaping

---

96  Ibid., 355.

97  Robert Chisholm, "בשר," *NIDOTTE*, 1:778.

his people in much the same way as the potter molded the clay in Jeremiah 18:1-6.

Divine sovereignty over his creation is a reality that should not be ignored. Some use the idea of "coercion"[98] to describe God's activity here. It would appear to this commentator that the emphasis should be placed, rather, on God's "redemptive" activity. As God faithfully kept his covenant with Israel, so would he fulfill his creative plan for her among the nations, so as to fulfill Exodus 19:5-6.

Ultimately, the Jews in Babylon transitioned from the earlier hope of an imminent return to an acceptance of God's timeline. With this realization of a longer stay in Babylon came new uncertainties. For example, there was the fear that the next generation might succumb to the pressures of assimilation. David Freedman captured the anxiety that existed within the exile community:

> The existence of a generation born and raised outside of Palestine brought about the possibility of complete assimilation to Mesopotamian culture and ultimate loss of the Yahwist heritage. The first generation could cohere on the basis of memories; the second generation needed a more formal principle of organization. To be sure, the need did not appear suddenly; the exiles had already asked Ezekiel, 'How can we live?' (Ezek. 33:10).[99]

---

98    Block, *Ezekiel 25-48*, 356.

99    David Noel Freedman, "Son of Man, Can these Bones Live?" *Int* 29 (1975): 181.

Freedman concludes that the second and following generations survived due to the existence of a "new organizing principle" within the community. He says, "The new organizing principle of Judahite religion was canon."[100]

Before considering the place of canon among the Jewish exiles, it is important to recognize the realities that these people faced. Jill Middlemas in her book, *The Templeless Age*, summarizes conditions that confronted the captives:

In Babylon, the community was faced with great loss: the loss of the homeland, the loss of leadership, the loss of cultural factors, the loss of the temple, and the loss of family members. Cast among a number of other peoples also removed from their homeland to Babylon, Judah's elite reassessed their religion and community. The fact that the Judahites were relocated together in communities enabled them to adapt creatively to their situation by establishing strategies to foster social cohesion and group identity.[101]

Amidst all the loss, the Jewish or Hebrew identity was still maintained within the community. They were still God's covenant people.

As pointed out above by Freedman, canon became the central unifying force around which the Jewish community organized itself. The writings that were broadly recognized as authoritative became the standard by which the community lived. Consequently, even without a temple or sacrificial system, the Jewish population

---

[100]   Ibid.

[101]   Middlemas, *Templeless Age*, 25.

in Babylon began to thrive. Signs of their spiritual life will be examined in the next chapter.

Still, this is not to suggest that the early years in Babylon were easy. In fact, the text of Ezekiel 37 describes the whole house of Israel as having died. It was only by God's direct intervention that this nation was resurrected and restored to life.

## Ezekiel 37

In Ezekiel 37, the prophet is taken by God's Spirit into a valley filled with dry bones. These bones are identified by God as "the whole house of Israel" (v. 11). Here, Ezekiel witnesses the miraculous resurrection of Israel. Referring to this vision, H. McKeating comments:

> This is the image. The reality that it symbolizes is of a nation that has lost all the attributes of nationhood. The people have lost king and political independence. They have lost temple and national cult. They have been taken away even from their land. All these things were the subject of the most solemn divine promises, and the promises have apparently gone for nothing.

> They are reduced to scattered communities (a dismembered body) in a foreign land with a powerful and overbearing culture to which they face all the pressures to assimilate.

> They know of the example of what happened over a century earlier to their compatriots of Northern Israel, exiled by

the Assyrians. They never returned, and lost their identity in the melting pot of Mesopotamia.

And in Ezekiel 37 the prophet has a vision that even from such a position restoration, resurrection is possible.[102]

That God was doing something miraculous at that moment in history and through the agency of his prophet is evidenced through Ezekiel's active participation in the resurrection process. Again McKeating says,

The restoration of the bones to life only happens, and happens in at least two stages, *at the instigation of Ezekiel himself.* . . . Life returns to the bones *when Ezekiel prophesies:* the *rûah* returns and reinvigorates the corpses *when Ezekiel prophesies to the rûah.*[103]

God's summary of what he was doing through this incredible event is found in v. 14: "I will put my Spirit in you and you will live, and I will settle you in your own land. Then you will know that I the Lord have spoken, and I have done it, declares the Lord."

Here, the Spirit of God works through the prophetic word of Ezekiel in such a manner that the nation of Israel is reconstituted as a living entity. The actions portrayed here reenact the activity of God's Spirit that occurred in the original creation (see Gen 2:7). Ezekiel watches as God's Spirit regathers, restructures, and then breathes life into Israel. Through the Spirit's re-creative work, the nation was in reality reborn.

———————————

[102]   H. McKeating, "Ezekiel the 'Prophet like Moses'?" *JSOT* 61 (1994): 105.
[103]   Ibid., 106.

God's Spirit moved in a sovereign, life-giving manner. Daniel Block captures the significance of the Spirit's work:

No text in the entire OT portrays the vivifying power of the divine spirit as dramatically as 37:1-14. The unit is dominated by the tenfold recurrence of the *Leitwort rwḥ* . . . .

The sixfold clustering of *rwḥ* in vv 8b-10a suggests that we have now arrived at the heart of the unit. The solution to the absence of the *rwḥ* is announced in v 9: "Prophesy to *hrwḥ*; / Prophesy, mortal. / Announce to *hrwḥ*: / Thus has the Lord Yahweh declared: / From the four *rwḥwt* come, O *rwḥ*! / Breathe into these slain that they may live." At the prophet's word the bodies are vitalized and, like Ezekiel himself in an earlier context (2:2; 3:24), they rise to their feet.

The play on *rwḥ* in v 9 is obvious. The *rwḥ* that the prophet has summoned is the breath of life, the life-force that animates all living creatures . . . . [From v. 14] we now learn that the bones do not simply represent dead persons in general but the nation of Israel, which Yahweh will bring back to life like people resurrected from their graves. They will be reclaimed as Yahweh's people and brought back to the land of Israel . . . . If the role of the prophet had really been to represent Yahweh, he should have breathed over them his own breath. But by merely adding the first-person singular suffix to *rwḥ* in v 14, Ezekiel produces an extremely significant shift in meaning. The *rwḥ* that will revitalize Israel is not the ordinary, natural life-breath common to all living things; it is the spirit of God himself. Only he is able to restore to life a nation that has been destroyed and whose remnant now languishes hopelessly in exile.[104]

This was truly a remarkable moment. Later in Block's article quoted above, he describes *rwḥ* as the power of God at work among humankind.[105]

Important questions arise from this passage: When did or will this intervention of God's Spirit occur, and how is one to understand the "newness" of the Spirit's activity in this passage?

In relation to the timing of Ezekiel 37:1-14, it is significant that while much of the material in the earlier chapters of Ezekiel anticipates a future work of God's Spirit among the nation of Israel (e.g. Ezek. 36:24-27), this passage functions in the historic present. To be sure, some scholars see the events presented here as occurring after the return. For example, Meindert Dijkstra believes that this passage "projects us into the sphere of the Jewish remnant that had survived the exile and, possibly, had returned to Jerusalem amidst the people of the land . . . ."[106]

The text, however, situates the Jews as living in exile. For example, after explaining to Ezekiel that the bones represented the "whole house of Israel" (v.11), God quotes the words of the exiles as saying, "Our bones are dried up and our hope is gone; we are cut off." This quote of the people fits the condition of living

---

[104] Block, "The Prophet of the Spirit," 37-38.

[105] Ibid., 49.

[106] Meindert Dijkstra, "The Valley of Dry Bones," in *The Crisis of Israelite Religion*, ed. Bob Becking and Marjo C.A. Korpel (Leiden: Brill, 1999), 125.

outside the land without hope of return. Their hope had been that Jerusalem would be saved and that a way of return would be provided. This had not happened. From a human standpoint, everything appeared hopeless. With Jerusalem lying in ashes and the temple destroyed, they felt totally "cut off." Any hope of return vanished (see Jer. 36:29). However, with all hope of return apparently gone, God promises to "bring [them] back to the land of Israel" (v.12).

## God's Spirit Intervenes

How would this be accomplished? The text suggests that God's Spirit would intervene in a new way. Is there textual evidence to substantiate the claim that God's Spirit was intervening in Israel's history in a way unknown in previous times? In answering this question several points relative to the Spirit are important.

First, the work of God's Spirit was certainly known in the earlier age as is evidenced in such passages as Psalm 51:12-13. Even the life of Saul illustrates the Spirit's activity, for after he was anointed king of Israel, the Spirit of the Lord came upon him and he prophesied (1 Sam. 10:6, 10). Additionally, the life of Ezekiel evidenced the powerful activity of God's Spirit (Ezek. 2:2; 3:24; 11:5).

Second, while the work of the Spirit was certainly known in previous times, his activity in bringing national Israel back from the dead was something profoundly new. As noted above, this work paralleled original creation. God, in fact, said, "O my people, I am going to open your graves and bring you up from them" (v.12).

Third, in speaking to the breath/spirit, Ezekiel is commanded by God to say, "Come from the four winds, O breath, and breathe into these slain, that they may live" (v.9). The "four winds" or "four winds of heaven" are most often used in describing God's scattering judgment on Israel or some other nation (see Jer. 49:36; Dan 11:4; Zech. 2:6). In Ezekiel 37, however, the breath is commanded to come from the "four winds." A mighty and powerful breath comes from the four winds breathing new life into the nation. This, then, details a reversal of God's previous judgment. There does not appear to be any preexilic equivalent to the Spirit's action here.

Fourth, God promised in the previous chapter (chap. 36) to give "to you" (pl.), *lkm*, "a new heart," *lb hdsh*, and to put "in the midst of you" (pl.), *bqrbkm*, "a new spirit," *ruh hdshh*, (36:26). The basic idea of the root, *qrb*, "denotes being or coming into the most near and intimate proximity of the object (or subject)."[107] The heart and spirit the Jews possessed in earlier times were clearly not adequate for what was needed now. Apart from a new work by God's Spirit within Israel, the results of any reform or change would fail. This would mean that these exiles would inevitably revert to their old ways.

To fulfill God's promise in relation to the Jews exiled in Babylon, a new transforming work by God's Spirit was required. In Jeremiah 24:7 God pledged, "I will give them a heart to know me, that I am the Lord. They will be my people, and I will be their God, for they will return to me with all their heart." This knowledge of God originated with God and was mediated to Israel through God's Spirit.

---

[107]  Leonard J. Coppes, "קרב," *TWOT*, 2:811.

Jesus' conversation with Nicodemus in John 3 seems particularly relevant to the promise of Jeremiah 24:7. In John 3:10, we note that Jesus was amazed by Nicodemus's ignorance of the working of God's Spirit. That Nicodemus did not understand the essential need of God's Spirit in the conversion process astounded Jesus. As Daniel Block states, "As far as Jesus is concerned, he is introducing nothing new. There can be little doubt that his statements here [in John 3:5-8] are based upon Ezekiel 36:25-29, a text with which the rabbi should have been familiar."[108]

Fifth, in v.14 God summarizes his future action on behalf of Israel as he describes the new condition that will exist when they return to the land. He says, "I will put my Spirit in you and you will live, and I will settle you in your own land. Then you will know that I the LORD have spoken, and I have done it, declares the LORD." The emphasis again is on the plural, you. The picture is of a people enlivened by God's Spirit back in the land of promise.

In addition to promising to give his people a new heart and a new spirit, God promised to purge his people "of those who revolt and rebel against me" (20:38). Not everyone taken to Babylon would be allowed to return to the land. Neither the false prophets nor those in the community living in rebellion to God would return. The returnees would be those who turned away from their rebellious ways and returned to the Lord (i.e., they repented).

Due to their repentance and the work of God's Spirit in their lives, a number of other changes would occur within the community. For example, Ezekiel 6:9 describes Israel's coming

---

[108] Block, "The Prophet of the Spirit," 40. Additionally, in v.25 God promised to cleanse Israel from all their "impurities and from all [their] idols." No longer would they be drawn to the idols of their neighbors.

to realize the gravity of her apostasy. The text says that "in the nations where they have been carried captive, those who escape will remember me-how I have been grieved by their adulterous hearts, which have turned away from me, and by their eyes, which have lusted after their idols." In describing this change of heart, Simon De Vries frames the transformation in the following manner: "Thus remembering her covenant obligations is to be an essential element in Israel's restoration, and this remembrance involves her repentance. Now she will turn in loathing from her wicked ways to serve Yahweh with a new heart" (see also 20:43 & 36:31).[109]

## Summary

To say that Jeremiah and Ezekiel lived through a truly remarkable moment in biblical history would be an enormous understatement. These two prophets witnessed cataclysmic events. Additionally, God opened a window into the future from where these prophets could see not only massive destruction but, looking beyond the devastation, a time of transformation and the restoration of Israel, when she would finally live up to God's original design for her.

Jeremiah and Ezekiel saw the worst of humanity and the best of God. On the one hand, these two prophets saw and experienced the evil and depravity of mankind in unimaginable ways. On the other hand, they witnessed the greatness and power of God working in and through the events of human history to accomplish his redemptive plan.

---

[109]   Simon J. De Vries, "Remembrance in Ezekiel," *Int* 16 (1962): 64.

For his part, Jeremiah foresaw God watching over and transforming the remnant in Babylon so that they could return to the land and live in the knowledge of God (Jer. 24:7). The spiritual and social fabric of those who returned would be different from the attitudes of those who went into captivity. This would be due to the work of God's Spirit leading them to repentance and enlivening them in Babylon. Further, Jeremiah spoke of a future larger return that would involve both Judah and Israel (Jer. 30:3; 31:8-14). This latter return would also be accompanied by repentance and would include a New Covenant functioning within a transformed society (Jer. 31:18-20, 31-34).

Ezekiel's experience was, in fact, different from Jeremiah's in that he lived and ministered among the exiles in Babylon.[110] On the one hand, he saw and experienced the apostasy and corruption that existed within Israel (Ezek. 3:7; 8-11; 33:32). More importantly, however, he witnessed and even played a part in the Spirit's activity of raising Israel from the dead (Ezek. 37:1-14). He too anticipated a near return when a transformed group would return and cleanse the land of "all its vile images and detestable idols" (11:18). Beyond that, however, Ezekiel foresaw a greater return that would involve God's cleansing of the nation, Israel and Judah being reunited, the establishment of an "everlasting covenant," a Davidic ruler, and God, himself, dwelling among his people (37:15-28). Eugene Merrill summarizes Ezekiel's vision of Israel's restoration:

At the beginning of his prophetic discourses, Ezekiel held out hope for some of the people-those, paradoxically,

---

[110]   In those early years he must have wondered about the goodness of these "good figs!"

fortunate enough to have been taken captive (Ezek. 6:8-10). Even in distant Babylonia the Lord would be their sanctuary (Ezek. 11:16), but they would return from there to the land of promise, rid it of all vestiges of idolatry, and undergo a radical renewal of heart (vv. 18-20). The Lord in response would establish with them an everlasting covenant, the nature of which the prophet elaborated later on (Ezek. 16:59-63; cf. 36:24-32).[111]

Neither Jeremiah nor Ezekiel could have imagined how God would ultimately fulfill his plans for Israel and for the nations—plans that continue to be fulfilled in our day.

---

[111]    Merrill, *Everlasting Dominion*, 545.

C H A P T E R  3

# PROPHETIC FULFILLMENT IN THE POSTEXILIC ERA: HAGGAI AND ZECHARIAH

As noted in the previous chapter, the late preexilic era was marked by widespread apostasy and moral corruption within Judean society. Details concerning this apostasy are described in such texts as Jeremiah 2, where God says, "My people have committed two sins: They have forsaken me, the spring of living water, and have dug their own cisterns, broken cisterns that cannot hold water" (v.13), and, "For you have as many gods as you have towns, O Judah" (v.28b).

In the years prior to Jerusalem's final destruction, both Jeremiah and Ezekiel went through suffering and rejection. While Ezekiel might not have experienced the verbal and physical opposition that was so much a part of Jeremiah's life, his words went largely unheeded during the early years of exile. The response of the exiles to Ezekiel's words is captured in the text, "Indeed, to them you are nothing more than one who sings love songs with a beautiful voice and plays an instrument well, for they hear your words but do not put them into practice" (33:32).

However, God assured Ezekiel that the people would eventually recognize him as God's spokesman, saying, "When all this [the prophetic pronouncements concerning Jerusalem's destruction] comes true—and it surely will—then they will know that a prophet has been among them" (v.33).

Unfortunately, the Bible provides few details relative to the spiritual life of the exiles in Babylon between the fall of Jerusalem and the well-known decree of King Cyrus. Was there widespread repentance within the Jewish community in Babylon? Further, was God fulfilling the promise he made in Jeremiah 24:5-7 in relation to these exiles? If so, in what ways did Judah's time in Babylon serve as an historic turning point for this remnant? Further, if a genuine turning to Yahweh did occur during this era, then one would expect to find evidence of this in the postexilic writings. This chapter and the next will examine four postexilic texts, seeking evidence that a spiritual transformation occurred in Babylon, thereby fulfilling the prophecy of Jeremiah 24.

The early postexilic era was marked by important people and events. Two major events of this era were the rebuilding of the temple and the reconstruction of the wall around Jerusalem. It is widely accepted that the temple was rebuilt during the reign of King Darius, whereas the wall was built during the reign of Artaxerxes I.[112] God used the prophets Haggai and Zechariah as his primary spokesmen to the people during the construction of

---

[112] Two helpful studies that analyze the chronology of these two eras are: Peter R. Ackroyd, "Two Old Testament Historical Problems of the Early Persian Period," *JNES* 17 (Jan., 1958) and A. Philip Brown II, "Nehemiah and Narrative Order in the Book of Ezra," *BSac* 162 (April-June 2005).

the temple. His words to the people of this era are recorded in Haggai and Zechariah 1-8.[113]

The wall was built years later. During this later era, God spoke to his people through Ezra and Nehemiah. Both of these men were uniquely prepared and qualified to lead and direct the remnant of Jews living in and around Jerusalem as the people worked on the wall and reestablished their relationship with Yahweh.

## Prophetic Fulfillment in Haggai

This section will research the following question: Does the text of Haggai provide demonstrable evidence for the thesis that a spiritual transformation occurred among the Jews in Babylon such that the *golah*, those Jews who returned from exile, were markedly different from their preexilic forefathers? If so, in what specific ways does the text demonstrate this transformation?

After providing the historic setting for his message and addressing the two leaders in Jerusalem (v.1), the prophet Haggai begins to critique the situation that existed in Judea (vv.2-6). He notes that the *golah* had concluded that the time was not yet right to resume the task of reconstructing the temple (v. 2). God, however, rejected this conclusion and challenged them to take up the rebuilding task immediately (v.8).

Professor Mark Boda describes Haggai's rhetoric by noting that "the phrase (על) שימו לבבכם [*shimu lbbkm ('l)*] (1:5, 7; 2:15, 18) is

---

[113]   The dating as to the writing of Zechariah 9-14 is uncertain and the focus is no longer on the rebuilding of the temple. Therefore, as noted in the previous chapter, these chapters will not be included in this study.

unique to Haggai. This idiom calls the audience to deep reflection over past behavior and experience. Its occurrence in 1:5 and 7 creates an envelope around the exposure of past experience."[114] This phrase, "Give careful thought (to your ways)," followed by a description of a life of frustration, was designed to challenge the people to rethink their decision to postpone rebuilding the temple.

There is a wordplay in the text that adds emphasis to God's message. Lisbeth Fried describes this wordplay as follows,

Haggai asks: "Is it a time for you yourselves to live in your paneled houses, while this house is a ruin? . . . Go up to the mountain and bring wood and build the house, so that I may take pleasure in it and be glorified, says YHWH" (Haggai 1:4, 8).

In other words, you live in paneled houses, but this house still lies unfinished, uninhabitable. Go to the mountain and get wood for the paneling, and finish the house. Haggai puns on the word חרב [*hrb*] translated here as "ruins." God's house is a ruin, so God calls ruin upon the land.

"And I have called for חרב [*hrb*] (a ruin, dryness, drought) on the land and the hills, on the grain, the new wine, the oil, on what the soil produces, on human beings and animals, and on all their labors" (Hag. 1:11).[115]

---

[114] Mark J. Boda, "Haggai: Master Rhetorician," *TynBul* 51, no. 2 (2000): 300.

[115] Lisbeth S. Fried, "The House of the God Who Dwells in Jerusalem," *JAOS* 126, no.1 (2006): 100.

How did the people respond to this exhortation? How did their response compare to the way their preexilic forefathers responded to God's word? Judah's preexilic attitude to the word of God is summarized by Isaiah saying, "For when I called, no one answered, when I spoke, no one listened" (Isa. 66:4). The height of rebellion against the word of God is illustrated in the life of King Jehoiakim as the words of Jeremiah's scroll are read to him. (Jeremiah 36) The text says, "Whenever Jehudi had read three or four columns of the scroll, the king cut them off with a scribe's knife and threw them into the firepot, until the entire scroll was burned in the fire" (v.23). From the king down to the common people, no one revered the word of God. In contrast, Haggai's text says that Zerubbabel, Joshua, the high priest, and "the whole remnant of the people obeyed the voice of the Lord their God . . . . And the people feared the Lord" (v.12). The positive response is emphasized by the placement of the verb "obey" at the beginning of the sentence: *vshm'*, "And he obeyed."[116]

The word *shm'* carries the primary sense of hearing sounds with the ear. However, K. T. Aitken provides this insight: "In a variety of contexts, *šm*`` denotes listen to, heed by acting upon, or putting into practice what has been said."[117] This response is reinforced by the statement and action that follow. As noted above, the verse ends, "And the people feared the Lord."

---

[116]   One might assume that the verb points only to Zerubbabel's obedience, but as Pieter Verhoef notes, "In Hebrew the predicate preceding two or more subjects frequently agrees in gender and number with the first and nearest subject." Pieter A. Verhoef, *The Books of Haggai and Malachi*, The New International Commentary on the Old Testament (Grand Rapids: Wm. B. Eerdmans Publishing, 1997), 80.

[117]   K. T. Aitken, "שמע," *NIDOTTE*, 4:180.

The word "fear," *yr'*, carries important theological meaning. Andrew Bowling states that the "biblical usages of *yārē'* are divided into five general categories: 1) the emotion of fear, 2) the intellectual anticipation of evil without emphasis upon the emotional reaction, 3) reverence or awe, 4) righteous behavior or piety, and 5) formal religious worship."[118]

The fear described here was connected with their obedience and also with the realization that they had been living in disobedience. These Jews had been putting their interests above those of Yahweh. Again Pieter Verhoef writes, "To obey the word of the Lord is to acknowledge one's own sinfulness and condemnation. Leaders and people alike became aware of the fact that the drought was due to God's judgment, because they sinfully withheld the honor that was due to him."[119]

Upon hearing this word from God the people recognized their self-centered living. This awareness led to repentance and a change of heart. The phrase, "And the people feared the Lord," summarizes this transformation in the thinking of the people. Their eyes were opened. They responded correctly.

At this point the returnees were brought back to their earlier hope. It seems that they had returned from exile anticipating a glorious life back in the land, only to encounter hardship and opposition. Unanticipated trouble had given rise to retreat and

---

[118] Andrew Bowling, "ירא," *TWOT*, 1:399. There is a marked contrast here between the reaction of these postexilic Jews and their preexilic ancestors. Of the latter, God said: "[They] have no awe of me" Jer 2:19. The Hebrew word for "awe," phd, carries the sense of "fear" or "dread." This was lost within the preexilic community.

[119] Verhoef, *Haggai and Malachi*, 83.

self-focused living. Consequently, life became even more difficult because the blessing of God was not upon them.

What was God calling them to do? First, they were to reflect on their circumstances. Second, they were to respond with obedience to God's command and restart the building project. This they did (v.12).

To this change of heart God responded with a simple but profound message: "I am with you." Additionally, God "stirred up the spirit" of Zerubbabel, Joshua, and the people so that they would act. The verb "to stir up," *'ur*, is used here in the causative Hiphil. Victor Hamilton states,

> If frequently God is the object of the [verb] when it is in the [qal], then as frequently he is the subject of the vb. when it is in the [hiphil]. That is to say, God not only is aroused to action, but arouses others to action. This idea is especially prominent when *rûaḥ* is the object of the vb.

> For example, Hag. 1:14 states that "the Lord stirred up the spirit of Zerubbabel . . . and the spirit of the whole remnant . . . [and they] began to work on the house of the Lord." So when used with *rûaḥ*, the [hiphil] of `wr means to arouse to action. Normally there is a political context for the activity in question.[120]

---

[120]   Victor P. Hamilton, "עור," *NIDOTTE*, 3:357.

Further insight comes from the commentary by Taylor and Clendenen:

> The verb `ûr, 'to stir up,' draws on the imagery of sleepiness. Like those roused from slumber to participate in activity from which they otherwise would have been absent, so these people had been roused from their spiritual inattentiveness to participate in the urgent task before them.[121]

To this Taylor and Clendenen add,

> The focus of the Lord's ministry to them is centered on their spirits. 'Spirit' (*rûaḥ*) in the Hebrew Bible can mean many different things (e.g., breath, breeze, wind, the human spirit, God's spirit). Here the word is used of God's arousing the human frame of mind to important activity, namely, the work on the temple.[122]

What is significant in the present text is not only God's direct access to the human spirit, which he always has, but the faith response of these Jews. Their response reflects God's previous work in their hearts. Verhoef provides a helpful insight:

> It is worthwhile to note that the stirring up of the spirit of the people to rebuild the temple has had its own history. It already began when the first exiles returned to their country. In Ezra 1:5 it is stated that the community and the

---

[121] Taylor and Clendenen, *Haggai, Malachi*, 143.

[122] Ibid.

religious leaders along with "everyone whose spirit God had stirred *[`ûr]*," prepared to go up and build the house of the Lord in Jerusalem. It is, therefore, a comforting thought that God's initiative to 'move' the hearts and spirits of his people to become active in his service does not vanish or diminish in the course of time. He does not abandon his work![123]

Further, God sovereignly continued to work in the hearts of his people. Again Verhoef writes, "Behind the willing response of both leaders and people was the silent working of the Lord, creating a willing attitude by his Spirit, with reference to Zech. 4:6: 'Not by might nor by power, but by my Spirit,' says the Lord Almighty."[124]

That this spiritual relationship between God and his people was quite fragile is highlighted in the first part of chapter 2. There God proactively asks a series of questions: "Who of you is left who saw this house in its former glory? How does it look to you now? Does it not seem to you like nothing?" (v.3)

Ezra provides insight into the various reactions expressed by those present when the foundation of the Second Temple was laid. He notes that among those shouting for joy were also those weeping as they remembered the glory of the previous temple. He says, "No one could distinguish the sound of the shouts of joy from the sound of weeping, because the people made so much noise. And the sound was heard far away" (Ezra 3:13).

---

[123]  Verhoef, *Haggai and Malachi*, 87. Much as believers today, from time to time, need a fresh stirring of God's Spirit in their lives, these people needed to be spiritually revived, not resaved.

[124]  Ibid.

Still, God was pleased with the willing response and efforts of his people. This is evidenced in his repeated promise to be with them (Ezra 2:4) and in his words, "This is what I covenanted with you when you came out of Egypt. And my Spirit remains among you. Do not fear" (2:5). In this last verse God connects his past faithfulness to Israel with their present condition. The use of the feminine participle, *'mdt,* "remains," points to the ongoing state of God's presence residing with his people. God puts no time limit or restriction on his continued presence with his people. With the two promises, "I am with you" and "my Spirit remains among you," God's people are assured of "God's guiding, sustaining, and abiding presence among leaders and people. They can rely on the Lord."[125]

Additionally, the use of the word *'md,* "remain" or "stand," may have reminded these Jews of how Yahweh delivered them from Egyptian bondage. This is due to the fact that when *'md* is used in its nominal form it can describe a "pillar" or "column."[126] Ronald Allen notes that this word was used to describe "the mysterious pillar of cloud that Yahweh would manifest himself before Moses (Num 12:5; Deut 31:15), and this mysterious manifestation in cloud, smoke, and fire was never forgotten by Israel (e.g. Neh. 9:12)."[127]

In examining the remainder of Haggai's text, several important observations deserve comment. First, the community to which Haggai spoke still faced the problem of sin or "uncleanness" (vv.10-14). The sin problem was not eradicated. Priests were still needed to make decisions regarding defilement. Commenting on Haggai 2:10-14, Janet Tollington makes the following observation,

---

[125]  Ibid., 101.

[126]  Francis Brown, *The New Hebrew and English Lexicon* (Boston: Houghton, Mifflin and Company, 1983), 764-765.

[127]  Roland B. Allen, "עמד," *TWOT,* 2:675.

In this passage, which is a conflation of the commission given to Haggai as well as an account of its fulfillment, the priests are asked to give a ruling, or torah, on matters of holiness and uncleanness. The answers given are then related to the condition of the community being addressed by Haggai in accordance with Yahweh's word to him.[128]

Some, like Paul Redditt, have concluded that in this passage Haggai was not speaking of the people, but rather was saying that it was the Temple that was defiled.[129] While this is an interesting explanation, God certainly could have stated this in a much simpler and less veiled manner. Additionally, v. 14 connects the defilement problem directly to "this people" and "this nation."

Another solution, proposed in John Bright's commentary, was that this prohibition "[regarded] contact with the native population as a contamination, urged that it be stopped altogether (Hag. 2:10-14)."[130] As such, this oracle served as a warning to the *golah* concerning the problem of intermarriage with the local pagan population, a problem that was to resurface during the ministries of Ezra and Nehemiah. While the interpretation of this passage (vv.10-14) is not simple, what can be said is that the problem of defilement continued to be a problem within the postexilic Jewish community.

---

[128] Janet A. Tollington, *Tradition and Innovation in Haggai and Zechariah*, (Sheffield: Sheffield Academic Press, 1993), 80.

[129] Paul L. Redditt, *Haggai, Zechariah, Malachi*, The New Century Bible Commentary (Grand Rapids: Wm. B. Eerdmans, 1995), 28.

[130] John Bright, *A History of Israel* (Philadelphia: Westminster Press, 1981), 368.

Next, after pointing to the reality of unfavorable agricultural conditions that existed for these Jews (vv.15-19a), God suddenly and unexpectedly promised to reverse this situation, saying, "From this day on I will bless you" (v.19b). God's blessing or favor was exactly what this remnant of Jews longed to experience.

According to Harry Mowvley, "There is nothing vague about blessing in the Old Testament. Fertility, prosperity in anything to which the blessed one puts his hand, well-being, riches, crops and the presence of God or His Spirit—these form its content."[131] The blessing these Jews longed for was understood in concrete and tangible terms. The covenant curses from earlier disobedience were now removed. God's blessing or favor was withdrawn from an earlier generation (see Jer. 3:3). As William Urbrock notes, "Blessing plays little role in the preexilic prophets, although curses are present."[132] This was caused by the defection of the Jews away from Yahweh and His covenant. Therefore the prophets pronounced words of judgment. One visual and verbal curse was delivered by Jeremiah. In chapter 19 he "smashed a pot in the presence of elders and senior priests while delivering a divine message that Jerusalem and its inhabitants were about to be broken by their enemies (Jer. 19:1-13) and would become (cursed) objects of hissing (v. 8; cf. Jer. 29:18)."[133] This earlier action taken by Jeremiah added to the significance of the blessing promised in

---

[131] Harry Mowvley, "The Concept and Content of 'Blessing' in the Old Testament," *BT* 16, no. 2 (April 1965): 79.

[132] William J. Urbrock, "Blessing and Curses," *The Anchor Bible Dictionary*, ed. David Noel Freedman (New York: Doubleday, 1990), 1:758.

[133] Ibid., 756. While on the one hand God judged his people and removed them from the land, his ultimate goal for them was redemptive, not destructive. In Babylon God watched over them for their good.

Haggai 2. These Jews had lived under this curse for some seventy or more years. Now, a major change was taking place. God said, "From this day on I will bless you" (v. 19).

This promise of blessing was given within the context of God's covenant with Israel (v. 5). Despite Israel's apostasy, Yahweh remained faithful to his promise. He was now promising to bless the *golah*. Even with the ongoing defilement problem, God in his grace promised to bless his people.[134]

As noted above, the blessing of God upon the nation had been lost years earlier (see Jer. 16:5). Even during the life of King Josiah, the last good king, one does not find reference to blessing upon his reign, only the restraint of inevitable judgment. Also, in the writings of the prophets, Isaiah, Jeremiah, and Ezekiel, blessing was primarily spoken of or used in a prophetic manner or at times in a general or proverbial sense. For example, in Jeremiah 17 the text states, "Cursed is the one who trusts in man . . . ," and then says, "But blessed is the man who trusts in the Lord" (vv. 5-7).

What is certain is that these words of Haggai served as a powerful public declaration to the *golah* that they had regained favored status with Yahweh. This blessing would provide the power needed to succeed in their activities. It would also

---

134   A textual question arises here as to the object of the blessing. The verb form used is the Imperfect piel and is employed without a direct object. It says, "I will bless," אברך. While the piel often acts to strengthen a qal verb, here according to Allen Ross, "a verb that is intransitive or stative in the qal may be given a transitive force in the piel." Literally, then, the promise of verse 19 says, "From this day, I will bless" with the implied "you." Allen P. Ross, *Biblical Hebrew* (Grand Rapids: Baker Book House, 2001), 196.

motivate them to live lives consistent with God's covenantal commands. This shift can be viewed as an historic reversal. For seventy years the land was under God's judgment, but now God was fulfilling his promise: "When seventy years are completed for Babylon, I will come to you and fulfill my gracious promise to bring you back to this place" (Jer. 29:10). God did not bring them back under judgment, though they did not experience his full blessing until they made significant progress on the temple.

Finally, understanding Zerubbabel's place in the fulfillment of prophecy is challenging. In Zechariah 4 his leadership in the rebuilding of the temple was guided by God (vv.7-10a) and specifically empowered by God's Spirit (v.6). The situation, however, is quite different in Haggai 2:20-23.

The passage in Haggai begins with the words, "The word of the Lord came to Haggai a second time on the twenty-fourth day of the month." This was the day "when the foundation of the Lord's temple was laid" (Hag. 2:18). This was a very significant day! As Meyers and Meyers note, "Throughout the ancient Near East the day of laying the foundations, or of the symbolic relaying of foundations in the case of a temple restoration, was a moment of particular importance."[135] Jerusalem must have been overflowing with people who had come for this celebration.

On this day, not only was there a ceremony marking the completion of the foundation, but God spoke. Haggai, in fact, received two messages from God that day. The first was God's word of blessing to the people, while the second was God's message to Zerubbabel (2:21-23). The oracle to Zerubbabel focuses on the future, to a time when Yahweh will abruptly intervene in

---

[135] Meyers and Meyers, *Haggai and Zechariah 1-8*, 81.

human history. It recalls Jeremiah's oracle against Babylon (see Jer. 51:20 f.). It also includes typical Day of the Lord wording (see Zeph. 1:14-18).

What do these messages to and about Zerubbabel mean? First, according to Meyers and Meyers, they meant "[T]he reestablishment of the kingship of God and not of man."[136] There is no hint in Haggai or Zechariah that a Davidic king would soon be reestablished on the throne. However, in the future there will be a time when Yahweh intervenes in human history to establish his theocratic rule. At that time this "Zerubbabel" will participate in God's administration of the nations as His signet ring.[137] God has a present plan for Zerubbabel, but an even greater plan for the future.

In this passage there is also a strong undercurrent of reversal. The promise of God in v.23 resonates back to the curse placed on Jehoiachin in Jeremiah 22. Zerubbabel, as Sara Japhet argues, was a direct descendant of Jehoiachin and in the line of David.[138] In the Jeremiah passage God says, "As surely as I live, even if you, Jehoiachin son of Jehoiakim king of Judah, were a signet ring on my right hand, I would still pull you off" (v.24). In Haggai 2, God has a message to Zerubbabel: "On that day, I will take you, my servant Zerubbabel son of Shealtiel and I will make you like my signet ring, for I have chosen you" (v.23). The curse placed on

---

[136]  Ibid., 82.

[137]  The words spoken here appear to have marked a major reversal to God's earlier judgment on Jehoiachin (Jer. 22:24), Zerubbabel's grandfather (see I Chron. 3:17-19).

[138]  Sara Japhet, "Sheshbazzar and Zerubbabel—Against the Background of the Historical and Religious Tendencies of Ezra-Nehemiah," *ZAW* 94 (1982): 71.

Jehoiachin was reversed in Zerubbabel. David Petersen identifies this day as a turning point.[139]

In writing about this passage Verhoef states, "In Zerubbabel, Haggai detected the *rector designatus* of God. Thereby he has legitimized the promise of the prophecy in 2 Samuel 7 concerning 'the house of David,' in a time when the idea of a Davidic king seemed to have been disregarded."[140] Therefore, the promise to Zerubbabel serves to connect God's ancient promise made to David with a future fulfillment. God remembers his promises.

In summary, in the text of Haggai there are signs of prophetic fulfillment and spiritual renewal being realized among the *golah*. The people responded to God's word spoken to them through Haggai and began to rebuild the temple. God's Spirit moved and remained among this remnant, and God's blessing returned to these people. Finally, the book ends with an anticipation of future and greater fulfillment with God's promise to Zerubbabel.

## Prophetic fulfillment in Zechariah

This next section of the study will continue to examine the spiritual life of the *golah* during the early years of King Darius's reign using insights gleaned from the Book of Zechariah. After years of hardship and frustration, some twenty years after the original return, what was the spiritual condition of the people in the land? John Bright has suggested:

---

[139] David L. Petersen, "Zerubbabel and Jerusalem Temple Reconstruction," *CBQ* 36 (1974): 369.

[140] Verhoef, *Haggai and Malachi*, 148.

[the community] was apparently divided into two ill-reconciled segments: those—mostly of the returning exiles—who were moved by lofty prophetic ideals and devotion to the faith and traditions of the fathers; and those—including probably the bulk of the native population—who had absorbed so much from the pagan environment that their religion was no longer Yahwism in pure form."[141]

If Bright is correct, this second group describes either Jews who had somehow escaped the Babylonian deportations and the exile to Egypt (Jer. 40-44), or who had returned from the surrounding nations. In either case, they probably continued in the apostasy of the preexilic era and had also intermarried with the local population. Clearly, the *golah* did not return to a healthy spiritual environment. They were met by political and spiritual opposition.

As noted earlier, the Book of Zechariah divides rather naturally at chapter 9. This study will not engage in the argument over dividing the book into First and Second Zechariah. For the purpose of analysis and in line with the internal dating, this study will focus only on the first eight chapters. Ben Ollenburger provides a helpful framework for the analysis of this first part of the book:

Within chaps. 1-8 a series of eight visions (1:7-6:15) is framed by a pair of sermons. The first of these sermons (1:1-6) is brief and retrospective. It reports a call to repentance, modeled on the preaching of the "former

---

[141]  Bright, *A History of Israel*, 368.

prophets" to the forebears, and the community's positive response. In style and vocabulary, vv.1-6 strongly resemble the second, much longer sermon that comprises chaps. 7-8. There, too, the preaching of the former prophets is of key importance, as is the refusal of the forebears to respond to their words. This lack of a response led to Yahweh's judgment, devastation, and the difficult circumstances from which Yahweh now promises to deliver the community (7:8-14; 8:1-8).[142]

Within this structure several themes emerge, three of which are particularly important to this study. The first theme to be noted is the theme of reversal. Again drawing from Ollenburger,

Reversal is itself a persistent theme of chaps. 1-8. It is expressed within the visions, where Yahweh will reverse the relative situations of Judah/Jerusalem and the nations (1:14-17) and in the long sermon, where the reversal of Judah's fortunes is joined with a reversal of Yahweh's stance toward the community (8:10-13).[143]

The second important theme upon which the idea of reversal depends is the theme of Yahweh's sovereignty. Here Ollenburger notes that every form of reversal, whether in an abstract or concrete form, is "subordinate to Zechariah's implicit and explicit

---

142    Ben C. Ollenburger, "Zechariah," in *NIB*, ed. Leander E. Keck (Nashville: Abingdon Press, 1996), 7:735-736.

143    Ibid., 739. This reversal needs to be understood in a decidedly positive sense, fulfilling the words of Jer 33:11, where God said, "For I will restore the fortunes of the land as they were before."

claim that Yahweh is 'lord of the whole earth' (4:14) . . . . Zechariah affirms the sovereignty of Israel's God."[144]

A third key theme presented by Zechariah, a theme that has an eschatological character, is that of a new world order. Again Ollenburger says,

> This newly ordered world has a social and moral character that contrasts with the past and the present. The land will be purged of its guilt (3:9) and of its wickedness (5:1-11). In the future, truthfulness, justice, and peace will characterize the people of Judah (8:10-19). Moral transformation is not the condition of God's return, but results from it.[145]

Using the three themes of reversal, divine sovereignty, and new world order, this study will seek to distinguish between historic spiritual transformation (i.e., transformation taking place within Zechariah's historic context) and transformation being projected into a future era, including the eschaton.[146]

The reversal theme is founded on Israel's repentance. For reversal to occur, Israel must repent. In the first sermon, God recounts the rebellious ways of the *golah's* forefathers. God says, "They would not listen or pay attention to me" (1:4). Of particular importance is the statement found in v.6b: "Then they repented and said, 'The Lord Almighty has done to us what our ways and practices deserve, just as he determined to do.'" This verse

---

[144] Ibid.

[145] Ibid.

[146] Due to the connectedness between reversal and divine sovereignty, these two themes will be handled together.

provides an important insight into what took place in Babylon. As Paul Redditt states,

> The disasters about which the preexilic ancestors had been warned came to pass. They had repented too late and could only confess that God had done to them as he had warned. They had no one to blame but themselves for what had happened. Though this verse did not actually mention the destruction of Jerusalem and the exile, those events were almost surely what was meant. Thus, the opening section of Zechariah functioned to exonerate God from any blame for the events of 586 and to fix the blame squarely on the ancestors themselves. This section also carried a warning to its postexilic audience: **do not be like your ancestors** (bold in text).[147]

As noted above, the idea of reversal depended on Yahweh's sovereign activity. Ezekiel anticipated that the exiles would eventually repent of their disloyalty to Yahweh. According to Ezekiel 14:5-6, God was engaged in "recapturing" the hearts of his people. A key element in this process involved bringing the people to repentance: "Repent! Turn from your idols and renounce all your detestable practices" (14:6). Only after deportation, the removal of all false hopes of return, and a life of exile that appeared to have no end, did they finally return to Yahweh. This repentance served as the basis for repatriation and also for a new relationship with Yahweh.

In the second sermon (Zech. 7-8), there is also a strong emphasis on the theme of reversal. God says, "You who now hear

---

[147] Redditt, *Haggai, Zechariah, Malachi*, 50-51.

these words spoken by the prophets who were there when the foundation was laid for the house of the Lord Almighty, let your hands be strong so that the temple may be built" (Zech. 8:9). These words accord with God's words spoken in Haggai 2:4: "Be strong, all you people of the land and work."

Here, as in Haggai 2:18, the laying of the foundation of the temple served as a turning point for the reversal of the social chaos that had previously existed in the Judean society. From both Haggai's and Zechariah's perspective, the laying of the temple's foundation marked a critical moment in the establishment of a new relationship between God and his people. In relation to rebuilding the temple, Ollenburger states, "Haggai's purpose is to persuade the people and their leaders to build God's house (Hag. 1:7). Zechariah's purpose is entirely compatible, but different."[148] He continues,

> Zechariah urges the people to continue heeding, trusting the prophetic word, whose instrument he is. Zechariah does not exhort the people to work on the Temple or on anything else; rather, he urges them to take the Temple's founding as a sign of the reversal to which he has been pointing since the beginning of chap. 8, and implicitly since his enigmatic remarks in 7:5-6. Zechariah did not regard temple construction as unimportant. Rather than regarding it as an obligation to be urged on his audience, he considered it the sign of a new day and a reason to believe the promises he makes, in continuity with earlier prophetic words.[149]

---

[148]   Ollenburger, "Zechariah," 796.

[149]   Ibid., 796-797.

Through the words of Zechariah, and specifically here in chapter 8, God makes it known that while the covenant curses had rested on the people and the land up to this point, they have now been lifted. A reversal has occurred. Here God says that "the seed will grow well, the vine will yield its fruit, the ground will produce its crops, and the heavens will drop their dew. I will give all these things as an inheritance to the remnant of this people" (v.12). (cf., Hag. 2:18)

These words reflect, at least in part, the fulfillment of the promises announced by Ezekiel: "I will bless them and the places surrounding my hill. I will send down showers in season; there will be showers of blessing. The trees of the field will yield their fruit and the ground will yield its crops; the people will be secure in their land" (34:26-27).

Three other important reversals are highlighted in chapter 8. The first involves Israel's place among the nations. With the loss of their king, their land, the temple, and the city of Jerusalem, they became "an object of cursing among the nations" (v.13). It seemed to the nations that Yahweh was weak, or that he had abandoned or even cursed his people. Now, however, God promises that through his sovereign power, his curse has been reversed and Israel will be a blessing, *brkh*, among the nations (cf. Gen 12:3).

God promises to reverse the curse on the land (vv.11-12) and then to make Israel a blessing. The promises, here, are presented in concrete rather than abstract terms. To be blessed and to be a blessing were something very real. Here the insight of John Oswalt is helpful:

Whatever may have been the ancient near eastern conception of the source of blessing, the OT sees God as the only source. As such he controls blessing and cursing

(Num 22f.). His presence confers blessing (II Sam 6:11-20), and it is only in his name that others can confer blessing (Deut 10:8, etc.). Indeed, God's name, the manifestation of his personal, redemptive, covenant-keeping nature, is at the heart of all blessing.[150]

The second reversal focuses on God's action toward his people. This reversal is found in vv.14-15 where God says, "Just as I had determined to bring disaster upon you and showed no pity when your fathers angered me . . . so now I have determined to do good again to Jerusalem and Judah. Do not be afraid." God here provides a summary of his actions. The word "determined," *zmm,* is used here twice. Herbert Wolf notes,

> *zāmam* is found only in the Qal stem. It is used mainly of the Lord carrying out his purposes in judgment against wicked nations or of wicked men who devise schemes against God and the righteous . . . . Zechariah 8:14-15 contrasts God's purpose to do harm with His new purpose to do good to Jerusalem."[151]

God's plans for his people, specifically those living in Jerusalem and Judah, have been reversed. Calamity or evil, *r',* is replaced by its antonym, *tob,* good (see Deut 30:19).

The third reversal has to do with fasts. The envoy sent from Bethel came with the question as to whether the people of Bethel should "mourn and fast in the fifth month" as had been the practice for so many years (Zech. 7:3). The reversal is found in

---

[150]  John N. Oswalt, "ברך," *TWOT,* 1:132.

[151]  Herbert Wolf, "זמם," *TWOT,* 1:244.

v.19 of chapter 8 where God says, "The fasts of the fourth, fifth, seventh and tenth months will become joyful and glad occasions and happy festivals for Judah." The sadness of the past has ended and is now replaced by joy. In comparing the initial question in 7:3 with the response in 7:5-6 and then the later response in 8:19, Ollenburger comments:

> Far from criticizing the practice of fasting, he adds two more fasts to the number he gave in 7:5, which was already double the number about which the Bethel embassy inquired. These additional fasts in the fourth and tenth months may be Zechariah's invention for rhetorical purposes, though Jewish tradition assigned them to different episodes in Jerusalem's destruction. Zechariah's point is that in the future fasting will be oriented, not to sin, divine wrath, tragedy, and devastation, but to celebration of what Yahweh has done for the house of Judah. There is a reversal of the very definition of fasting: not abstinence and mortification, but joy. It does not answer the Bethel embassy's inquiry: instead, it redefines the present.[152]

In v.19 the word "joy" is derived from the root *shush*, a word that according to Michael Grisanti serves as an "indicator of the status of Israel's covenant relationship [with Yahweh]."[153] As Judah's covenantal relationship with Yahweh is restored, their festivals will be marked by joy and gladness.

---

152   Ollenburger, "Zechariah," 798-799.
153   Michael A. Grisanti, "שוש," *NIDOTTE*, 3:1223.

## Zechariah's Visions

Reversal and divine sovereignty also play an important role in Zechariah's visions. For example, from God's response to the angel's inquiry in the first vision (Zech. 1:14-16), it is evident that the focus of God's attention has returned to Jerusalem. The angel asks the Lord: "Lord Almighty, how long will you withhold mercy from Jerusalem and from the towns of Judah, which you have been angry with these seventy years?" (1:12) From the angel's question, it appears that the prophesied seventy years of exile have reached fulfillment. In response God replies, "I am very jealous for Jerusalem and Zion . . . I will return to Jerusalem with mercy, and there my house will be rebuilt. And the measuring line will be stretched out over Jerusalem" (vv.14, 16). While God is sovereign over all the earth, his attention has returned to Jerusalem and his earlier judgment has been reversed. Prior to Jerusalem's destruction, God's wrath rested on the city and its leaders (see Jer. 24:8-10). Now, however, God's favor is extended to the *golah*.

As noted above, God said, "I am very jealous for Jerusalem and Zion" (Zech. 1:14). In chapter 8 he repeats his earlier statement: "I am very jealous for Zion; I am burning with jealousy for her" (v.2). Paul Redditt sees two ideas implicit in this second verse: "First, God's wrath will be poured [out] on Zion's enemies. Second, their punishment will allow Zion to receive the blessings God had in store for them."[154]

What immediately follows in chapter 8 is God's promise to return and dwell in Jerusalem. According to Victor Hamilton,

---

[154]   Redditt, *Haggai, Zechariah, Malachi*, 84.

the word *shkn* means "dwell, tabernacle."[155] Further, Hamilton notes that in comparing this word to its synonym *yāshab*, *shākan* "underscores the idea not of loftiness but of nearness and closeness."[156] God is committed to dwell with his people in the closest possible manner.

The impact of God's return and dwelling in Jerusalem will be that the city will be repopulated and the condition of *shalom* in its fullest sense will be extended to the entire population (vv.4-5). While aspects of this promise may have been fulfilled historically, vv.7-8 anticipate a future and greater fulfillment that will surpass anything that God's people could imagine (v.6).

Referring to this passage, Ben Ollenburger writes,

Just as the Lord is returning to dwell in Jerusalem, so also Yahweh will bring "my people" back to dwell there (vv.3, 8). Just as the restored city will be "faithful" and the mountain "holy," so also God's relationship with them will be restored, in faithfulness and righteousness (vv.3, 8; cf. Isa 48:1). The full covenant formula appears here: "they will be my people, and I will be their God." This pronouncement, too, is a reversal, from the mutually severed relationship (7:13) to its restoration in mutuality and integrity (8:8).[157]

Historically, God was committed to even greater restoration, for he makes a call to the Jews still living in exile to return to the land (Zech. 2:6-7). Along with this, God extends a warning

---

[155]  Victor P. Hamilton, "שכן," *TWOT*, 2:925.

[156]  Ibid.

[157]  Ollenburger, "Zechariah," 795.

to anyone who would touch his people (v.8). As Redditt says, "Whoever struck Judah was guilty of striking the **apple** of God's **eye**. The apple was the pupil, so whoever struck Judah was striking God in the pupil of his eye. The phrase connoted a very close relationship between God and his people" (bold in text).[158]

Turning next to the theme of a new world order, in the vision in chapter 2 God speaks of Jerusalem being "a city without walls" (v.4), and of God himself acting as "a wall of fire around it" (v.5). As David Petersen writes, "Zechariah reports that Yahweh will no longer be localized in his temple. Instead, Yahweh will be a wall of fire around the city."[159] As part of this new world order, God's presence will serve to protect the city and will also "be its glory within" (v.5b).

In the vision in chapter 3, Joshua, the high priest, is cleansed and commissioned. This cleansing and commissioning is then followed by more elements of the new world order. God says, "And I will remove the sin of this land in a single day. In that day, each of you will invite his neighbor to sit under his vine and fig tree" (vv.9-10). The new world order will be marked by peace and harmony in the land.

Chapter 3 can be understood as having both a near and a distant application for the Jews. The near application provided for the immediate restoration of Joshua's historic function as high priest serving within the community. James Vanderkam writes,

---

[158] Redditt, *Haggai, Zechariah, Malachi*, 50-51. It seems altogether possible that God's call to Jews still living in exile, here in Zechariah 2, may have been a factor in Ezra's decision to return to the land.

[159] David L. Petersen, "Zechariah's Visions: A Theological Perspective," *VT* 34, no. 2 (April 1984): 201.

As removal of his filthy garments represented the erasure of his guilt, so donning splendid high-priestly vestments meant that the cult, headed by the high priest, would once more effect its ancient goal of restoring the damaged relations between God and his people. It seems, too, that Joshua's new clothing marks the resumption of communication between God and the priest . . . Investiture of the high priest means the divine remembrance of his people and his regular communication with them.[160]

In this new world order, the high priest is called upon to play a key role in maintaining the spiritual health of the nation. At the same time, the final verses of the chapter include markers that serve to project ultimate fulfillment into the future. The first is found in God's promise in v.8: "I am going to bring my servant, the Branch." While commentators have suggested a variety of identities for this Branch, Vanderkam's definition is both simple and appropriate. He defines this Branch as "a Davidic heir."[161] This would apply to both Zerubbabel in 6:12 and to a future individual (e.g., a messianic figure) in the Davidic line.

A second future marker comes at the beginning of v.10: "In that day." This phrase often points to the distant future (see Isa. 11:10; 19:18, 19, 21, 23, 24; Ezek. 38:18). It does so here. In v.10, one finds a picture of Jewish neighbors sitting "under the vine and the fig tree." According to Ronald Youngblood, "To be able to sit under one's own vine and fig tree was to share God's blessings of peace, prosperity and security, whether in past remembrance (I Kings

---

[160] James C. Vanderkam, "Joshua the High Priest and the Interpretation of Zechariah 3," *CBQ* 53 (Oct. 1991): 568.

[161] Ibid.

4:25 [H 5:5]; see also I Macc. 14:12) or in future eschatological hope (Mic. 4:4; Zech. 3:10)."[162]

Therefore, chapter 3 can be understood as having application for spiritual restoration between God and his people both during the ministry of Zechariah and in a final fulfillment at the end of this age. Consequently, it can have application both to Judah in the past and to greater Israel in the future. This is also true for the oracles in Zech. 8:9-23, for they have application to the life situation that the *golah* experienced historically and also to what will happen in the future.

In summary, Zechariah 1-8 provides important insights into the themes of reversal, divine sovereignty, and God's new world order. There is often a free mixing of promises that can have both present (i.e., in Zechariah's day) and future application. According to chapter 1, the forefathers finally came to their spiritual senses and repented, acknowledging that Yahweh had done to them what their ways deserved (1:6b). A new day then began that led to the return of the *golah*. God's attention has now been turned back to Jerusalem and he promises to once again dwell among his people.

As noted above, the promises in chapter 8 appear to have both near and distant application. For the present, God promises to reverse the social chaos of the past, to end the covenant curses that were on the land, to establish a new relationship with his people, to return fertility to the land, and to transform the fasts from a time of sadness to a time of great joy.

---

[162] Ronald F. Youngblood, "תאנה," *TWOT*, 2:963.

CHAPTER 4

# PROPHETIC FULFILLMENT IN THE POSTEXILIC ERA: EZRA AND NEHEMIAH

## Prophetic Fulfillment in Ezra

In the next two sections attention turns to the time period when Ezra and Nehemiah lived and ministered in Jerusalem. This study will follow the traditional view that sees Ezra arriving in Jerusalem in approximately 458 B.C., in the seventh year of Artaxerxes, agreeing with Ezra 7:8.[163] This would put him in Jerusalem approximately thirteen years prior to Nehemiah's first trip to the city (see Neh. 1:1; 2:1).

This section of the study will first examine themes and then look for elements that relate to prophetic fulfillment and spiritual transformation. What themes are presented in Ezra's text, and how do they compare with the themes discussed in Haggai and Zechariah? Second, how did Ezra understand prophecy and its

---

[163] See Walter Brueggemann, *An Introduction to the Old Testament* (Louisville: Westminster John Knox Press, 2003), 363.

fulfillment relative to his return and to life and conditions in Jerusalem?

Ezra's text begins with the words of Cyrus, declaring that under divine authority he, Cyrus, has been appointed to build a temple in Jerusalem. This decree, however, is interpreted in the text of Ezra as directly attributable to the fulfillment of Jeremiah's prophecy (Ezra 1:1). Additionally, Ezra writes, "Then the family heads of Judah and Benjamin, and the priest and Levites—everyone whose heart God had moved—prepared to go up and build the house of the Lord in Jerusalem" (1:5). The verb "moved," *'ur*, used here and in 1:1, is the same verb used in Haggai 1:14 (see discussion of this word in Haggai section). The sovereign action of God moved Cyrus to make his decree. It also stirred a group of Jews to action, so that they returned to the land. Then, some twenty years later, God again moved the Jews to rebuild the temple.

About this verse (Ezra 1:5) Mervin Breneman writes, "God sovereignly uses his own people as well as foreign rulers (v. 1) to accomplish his will. Their purpose in going to Jerusalem also was God-centered: they went to build the house of the Lord."[164] Ezra understood that every aspect of the return had been carefully orchestrated by the sovereign hand of God, including the exact individuals who returned.

Further, Ezra highlights the action of reversal as a major part of the return. For example, the text says, "Moreover, King Cyrus brought out the articles belonging to the temple of the Lord, which Nebuchadnezzar had carried away from Jerusalem and had placed in the temple of his god" (Ezra 1:7). According to v.11, Sheshbazzar brought 5,400 articles of gold and silver with

---

[164] Mervin Breneman, *Ezra, Nehemiah, Esther*, The New American Commentary, 10 (Nashville: Broadman and Holman, 1993), 70.

him from Babylon to Jerusalem. These articles were returned to Jerusalem and eventually placed in Yahweh's temple.

However, an ongoing tension exists in the text. On the one hand, the return and the rebuilding of the temple are seen as divinely guided and orchestrated. On the other hand, every phase of rebuilding is challenged by the enemies of God's people. For example, in chapter 5 Ezra records events associated with the reign of King Darius. Through the encouragement of Haggai and Zechariah, the people take up again the work of rebuilding the temple. However, they are immediately challenged by the local leadership asking them for proof that they had the necessary permission to engage in this work (vv.3-4).

Due to the fact that this work had been stopped so many years earlier, this challenge may well have seemed insurmountable. The text, however, declares that "the eye of their God was watching over the elders of the Jews, and they were not stopped until a report could go to Darius and his written reply be received" (v.5). Charles Fensham discusses the significance of this verse:

> A good eye turned on someone means that special care is taken of a person or persons. A report was dispatched. The term for report, *ṭaʿmāʾ*, means full particulars on what was happening. The Jews were allowed to continue their work until an official document was received from the Persian king. This may be due to Tattenai's uncertainty as to what to expect of the new Persian king.[165]

---

[165]  F. Charles Fensham, *The Books of Ezra and Nehemiah*, The New International Commentary on the Old Testament (Grand Rapids: Eerdmans, 1982), 80.

Here, too, Ezra points to the theme of the sovereign hand of God actively involved in every detail of the work. To this Breneman adds,

> Ezra-Nehemiah constantly reiterates God's providence in the life of his people. The reestablishment of the covenant community was the result of a continuing series of God's providential acts . . . . God so guided Tattenai's attitude that he allowed the Jews to continue the construction until he could check with King Darius. In order to fulfill his purpose, God used and coordinated the preaching of the prophets, the work of the leaders, the determination of the whole community, and the decisions of "pagan" government officials.[166]

Ezra does not want the reader to miss the fact that God's hand was intricately involved in every detail of the building process. Still, in every aspect of the work progress was slow and the resistance was relentless.

Ultimately success was achieved under the guidance of godly men like Haggai and later Nehemiah, who remained focused on their goals. And while considerable attention was paid to the task at hand, for each of these leaders the spiritual condition of the *golah* was of primary importance.

Next, attention turns to the spiritual condition of the Jewish community in Judah at the time of Ezra and Nehemiah as it relates to prophetic fulfillment. As noted above, the Book of Ezra begins with God moving the heart of Cyrus to make his famous decree. The stage was set for the return.

---

[166] Breneman, *Ezra*, 108-109.

Following their journey, Ezra describes events associated with the arrival or the *golah* in Jerusalem: "When they arrived at the house of the Lord in Jerusalem, some of the heads of the families gave freewill offerings toward the rebuilding of the house of God on its site" (2:68). The phrase "they gave freewill offerings" is contained in the one Hebrew word *htndbu*. According to Leonard Coppes,

> The root *ndb* connotes an uncompelled and free movement of the will unto divine service or sacrifice . . . . The verb *nādab* occurs three times in the Qal and each time describes the inner state of those contributing to the construction of the tabernacle . . . . The rest of the occurrences are in the Hithpael and, hence, are reflexive. The building (I Chr 29:5) and rebuilding (II Chr 35:8; Ezr 1:6) of the temple elicited abundant voluntary giving and sacrifice (Ezr 3:5) from God's people.[167]

The text emphasizes that the hearts of God's people were fully committed to him (see Jer. 24:7). This was illustrated by their giving.

After listing those who returned (chapter 2), Ezra describes the first major community event to occur in Jerusalem, the Feast of Tabernacles, recorded in chapter 3. The text highlights several features in describing this event. It states that "the people assembled as one man in Jerusalem" (v.1). This gathering was marked by a spirit of unity.

Second, the faith and commitment to Yahweh of the leaders and the people are highlighted in the building of the altar. The text says that "despite their fear of the peoples around them, they

---

[167] Leonard J. Coppes, "נדב," *TWOT*, 2:554.

built the altar on its foundation and sacrificed burnt offerings on it to the Lord, both the morning and evening sacrifices" (v.3). Their commitment to worship and obedience was greater than their fear of their neighbors.

Third, the heart commitment of the *golah* is seen in their obedience to Torah. The next verse, v.4, records, "Then in accordance with what is written, they celebrated the Feast of Tabernacles with the required number of burnt offerings prescribed for each day." Of the three major festivals, Passover (*Pesach*), Pentecost (*Shavuot*), and Tabernacles (*Sukkot*), Tabernacles was the largest, particularly in relation to the number of required sacrifices.[168]

In addition, the people continued to present the required burnt offerings and sacrifices along with freewill offerings throughout the year (v.5). Mervin Breneman provides a valuable insight:

The community of Jews who returned from exile was careful to set up and continue (not just a momentary impulse) its worship according to Scripture. The heart that loves God desires to worship him in a way that pleases him. The people even "brought . . . freewill offerings to the Lord." The true worshiper is not miserly with God.[169]

---

[168] A general description of the Festival of Tabernacles is found in Lev. 23:33-43. The description of the required number of sacrifices, however, is recorded in Numbers 29. Beginning with day 1 they sacrificed 13 bulls, 2 rams, and 14 lambs. While the number of rams and lambs sacrificed each day stayed the same, the number of bulls sacrificed decreased by one on each of the seven days. Nevertheless, by the end of seven days they had sacrificed 70 bulls, 14 rams, and 98 lambs, all of the best of their flocks. This was not an insignificant offering for a group that had so recently returned from exile!

[169] Breneman, *Ezra*, 92-93.

Ezra 3 emphasizes that the people freely gave and that they were unified. Their unity resulted from their knowledge of and commitment to obey the Law of Moses. In this passage the people exhibit features of what was prophesied in Jeremiah 24:7: "They will return to me with all their heart."[170]

Chapter 6 records the completion of the temple followed by the celebration of Passover. Beginning with verse 20, the passage describes a community that conscientiously followed the law. The text says,

> The priests and Levites had purified themselves and were all ceremonially clean. The Levites slaughtered the Passover lamb for all the exiles, for their brothers the priests and for themselves. So the Israelites who had returned from the exile ate it, together with all who had separated themselves from the unclean practices of their Gentile neighbors in order to seek the Lord, the God of Israel. For seven days they celebrated with joy the Feast of Unleavened Bread, because the Lord had filled them with joy by changing the attitude of the king of Assyria, so that he assisted them in the work on the house of God, the God of Israel (vv. 20-22).

The text here describes a growing community of Jews committed to a life of obedience to the Law of Moses. The Passover

---

[170] This description of the hearts of the returnees may in some sense parallel God's "unique" view of Israel coming out of Egypt as described in Jer. 2:2-3: "I remember the devotion of your youth, how as a bride you loved me and followed me through the desert, through a land not sown. Israel was holy to the Lord, the firstfruits of his harvest." In both cases, there did exist a true element of love and devotion!

is celebrated not only by the *golah*, those who had returned from the exile, but by other Jews who had "separated themselves from the unclean practices of the Gentile neighbors in order to seek the Lord, the God of Israel." What is significant here is the importance placed within the community on the distinction between clean and unclean, because of the realization that contact with the unclean would defile the larger community.

"To separate," *bdl*, oneself in order "to seek," *drsh*, the Lord (i.e. to live in compliance with his will) became a distinguishing mark of the postexilic era (see the promise of Jer. 29:13). This was a marked change from the preexilic period. In describing the earlier sins of Jerusalem, God through Ezekiel said, "Her priests do violence to my law and profane my holy things; they do not distinguish between the holy and the common; they teach that there is no difference between the unclean and the clean; and they shut their eyes to the keeping of my Sabbaths, so that I am profaned among them" (22:26). The postexilic community was careful to distinguish the holy from the common.

It is noteworthy that "to separate," *bdl*, has its roots in the creation story. Cornelius Van Dam writes, "Judging from the usage of *bdl* elsewhere, its usage in Genesis should probably be understood in terms of separating what does not belong together and separating for a specific task."[171]

A further development of this idea can be found in the law. Here again Van Dam notes that "this vb. is used for the separation of the holy and the common, the clean and unclean. It was a key responsibility of the priests to distinguish between these . . . ."[172]

---

[171]  Cornelius Van Dam, "בדל," *NIDOTTE*, 1:604.
[172]  Ibid.

Finally, Van Dam applies this concept to the specific situation existing in postexilic Israel. He says,

> To maintain their identity as people of the Lord, Israel was called to be separate from the nations (cf. Deut. 7:1-6: Ezra 6:21, ni.). This demand included not marrying foreigners, and in Ezra's time separating oneself also meant breaking marriages with foreigners (Ezra 9:1-2, ni.; 10:11, ni.; cf. 2 Cor. 6:14). Those who did not want to cooperate with Ezra's efforts to cleanse the nation were to be excluded (*bdl*) or excommunicated from the assembly of the exiles (Ezra 10:8, ni.; cf. Matt. 18:17; 2 Thess. 3:14-15). Also all who were of foreign descent were excluded (*bdl*) from Israel (Neh. 13:3, hi.).[173]

God demands exclusive allegiance from those who would follow him. While there is the danger of pride and arrogance, there is at the same time a biblical mandate calling for separation from that which is unclean. As believers of all ages seek God and his will for their lives, they inevitably must separate themselves from those things that defile them.

In his description of this Passover celebration, Mervin Breneman writes,

> This verse [v.21] shows that there were Jews living in Judah other than the ones who returned from the exile. Apparently many had been assimilated with non-Jewish people who also lived there. The religious fervor of the returned exiles served to call these Jews back to the

---

[173] Ibid., 605.

religious and ethical norms of the Torah, the books of Moses. Ezra and Nehemiah may give the impression that the returned exiles were very exclusive, but at least they accepted the other Jews (who had not been in Babylon) when they made a definite decision to follow God according to the Torah traditions.[174]

The text states that the reason for separating themselves from the unclean practices of their Gentile neighbors was to "seek," *drsh*, the Lord, the God of Israel. Was the spiritual attitude or commitment exhibited by these Jews significantly different from that of an earlier generation, in particular, those living when Jeremiah and Ezekiel ministered? The answer appears to be an unqualified, yes.

The idea of an exclusive allegiance to Yahweh was at the heart of covenantal loyalty (see Exod. 20:3). Writing on the covenantal usage of the word *drsh*, David Denninger states,

The predominant use of *drš* describes humans either seeking God or inquiring of him for a specific answer. Sometimes *drš* involves a traditionally or legally established procedure. Seeking is a privilege and responsibility belonging to the covenant community; . . . Neglecting to seek Yahweh or seeking elsewhere breaks his covenant or a specific command. Only two Torah prohibitions use *drš*: Deut 18:11 (consulting the dead) and 12:30 (inquiring about the Canaanite gods).[175]

---

174    Breneman, *Ezra*, 121.
175    David Denninger, "דרש," *NIDOTTE*, 1:995.

Additionally, Denninger writes, "Ezra 6:21 uses *drš* (Yahweh) as the motive for separation from unclean practices; a sim. sense to Chron. *drš* (with Torah) means study, an emerging postexilic focus and identification of the faithful (7:10)."[176]

According to the writer of the Book of Chronicles, Saul's death was directly attributable to his seeking guidance from a medium and not from Yahweh: "Saul died because he was unfaithful to the Lord; he did not keep the word of the Lord and even consulted a medium for guidance, and did not inquire of the Lord. So the Lord put him to death and turned the kingdom over to David son of Jesse" (I Chron. 10:13-14).

During Ezekiel's ministry Yahweh condemned the Jews for seeking help from pagan sources and then coming and inquiring of him. For example, Ezekiel 20:31 says, "When you offer your gifts—the sacrifice of your sons in the fire—you continue to defile yourselves with all your idols to this day. Am I to let you *inquire* of me, O house of Israel? As surely as I live, declares the Sovereign LORD, I will not let you *inquire* of me" (italics added). Of major importance to Ezekiel's ministry was his unwavering condemnation of Israel's covenantal infidelity in seeking help from sources other than Yahweh.

A synonym of *drsh* is the word *bqsh*, "seek, look with care, petition." In the book of Ezra this second word is used to describe the actions of the Jewish community as Ezra and his fellow countrymen prepare to travel from Babylon to Jerusalem. Chapter 8 finds them assembling by the Ahava Canal in Babylon. It was during this time that Ezra recognized the dangers facing this group on their long journey and called for a fast (v.21). Verse 23 says: "So we fasted and petitioned (*nbqshh*) our God about this,

---

[176]  Ibid., 997.

and he answered our prayer." Chitra Chhetri's comments provide helpful insight:

> Moreover, the two words *bqš* and *drš* are used in synonymous parallelism in some passages. For example, in Deut 4:29 Moses speaks to Israel: "But if from there you seek (*bqš*) the Lord your God, you will find him if you look (*drš*) for him with all your heart and with all your soul." This is an exhortation of Moses to that generation and to the generation to come as a warning against the outcome of idolatry and subsequent returning to God with remorse for his mercy and forgiveness. Similarly in Jer 29:13, Jeremiah writes to all the exiles to submit to the Babylonian captivity as God's legitimate punishment for her apostasy and with penitence to return, asking for his restoration: "You will seek me (*bqš*) and find me when you seek (*drš*) me with all your heart."[177]

Given Ezra's broad knowledge of the Torah, it seems reasonable that he would be eager to see the promise of Deuteronomy 4:29 fulfilled by those returning to the land of promise. The text provides substantial evidence for the idea that Ezra and those traveling with him saw their return as a spiritual pilgrimage, fulfilling the promise of Deuteronomy 4:29 and Jeremiah 29:13. Consequently, the people willingly responded to Ezra's call to fast and petition God prior to leaving. This in turn gave rise to Ezra's summary description of their trip: "The hand of our God was on us, and he protected us from enemies and bandits along the way" (Ezra 8:31b).

---

[177]  Chhetri, "בקש," *NIDOTTE*, 1:721.

# Ezra and the Return to the Land

An important question arises at this point in the study: What kind of vision of Israel's future did Ezra anticipate as he prepared to return to the land? As he traveled from Babylon to Jerusalem, was he primarily envisioning the establishment of a strict theocratically-based postexilic community, as argued by Julius Wellhausen, or did he return with a grander vision based on prophetic fulfillment and Israel's eschatological hope?[178]

Additionally, how did Ezra understand Judah's time in Babylon? Was it primarily a time of discipline and loss? Or did he view this period of their history as principally redemptive? Had Yahweh graciously intervened in Israel's history to reverse her downward spiritual spiral with the goal of beginning a new work, a work marked by spiritual renewal based upon the twin pillars of repentance and Torah? Further, in his preparations and travels did Ezra find the Torah to be his primary source of both promise and instruction? Also, what prophetic value, if any, did he give to the return of the *golah* as part of God's ultimate plan of restoration and rule over Israel and the nations? These questions get to the heart of what took place among the Jewish exile community in Babylon.

Did God fulfill his promises given in Jeremiah 24:5-7 & 29:10-14? If so, Julius Wellhausen's argument that Ezra returned seeking to establish a rigid theocracy cannot be sustained.[179] If the Jewish community in Babylon experienced a profound repentance, one would anticipate that the people who emerged from such an experience would be marked by humility and spiritual zeal. A

---

178  Wellhausen, *Prolegomena*, 500

179  Ibid., 496

resulting strict legalism would seem incompatible with that type of experience.

Examination of Ezra's life and also his response to the problems he encountered upon his return, in particular the problem of intermarriage, should provide insight into the character of this man. Did the problems he encountered lead him to disillusionment and despair? Or was he motivated by a larger vision in regard to Israel's future such that even a partial fulfillment of God's promises provided him with a framework of hope and assurance for the future?

In an important article, J. G. McConville has argued that the books of Ezra and Nehemiah were "informed by prophecy—especially by the Books of Isaiah and Jeremiah—to a far greater extent than is usually thought."[180] For example, McConville finds extensive allusion to Jeremiah 31 in Ezra 7-9. He writes,

> As Jer. xxxi predicts the return of a remnant from a far land, so Ezra actually leads such a return. He has gathered the exiles (viii 15); he is confident that it is God who is the real deliverer and that he (God) leads them for their good (viii 22), and will protect them from the enemy (viii 22, 31); the destination is the holy place (ix 8, which refers to Jerusalem, and in Jer. xxxi 40 to an area adjacent to the city, from which presumably its holiness is derived).

> The similarity of theme and vocabulary strongly suggests that the Ezra memoir is deliberately modeled on the

---

[180]  J.G. McConville, "Ezra-Nehemiah and the Fulfillment of Prophecy," *VT* 36, no.2 (1986): 207.

prophecy in Jer. xxxi (which is not to suggest that it is merely a fiction devised on the basis of it) . . . .

The second striking affinity between the two passages is the fact that this theme of fulfillment (with "exodus" overtones in each case) is mitigated by one of repentance.[181]

What motivated Ezra to leave his familiar and secure surroundings in Babylon and travel for four months over dangerous territory, only to arrive in Jerusalem with its broken-down walls and its people living in distress? As suggested above, Ezra viewed his return through the grid of prophetic fulfillment. He understood his return as part of God's larger redemptive plan for Israel.

Evidence for this assertion can be found in the summary list of those who accompanied Ezra in the return. Ezra 7:7 says, "Some of the Israelites, including priests, Levites, singers, gatekeepers and temple servants also came up to Jerusalem in the seventh year of King Artaxerxes." Those listed played important roles in reestablishing and maintaining Israel's spiritual life.

They returned with their eyes fixed on God. This idea was predicted by the prophet Isaiah, who pictures this type of return:

In that day the remnant of Israel, the survivors of the house of Jacob, will no longer rely on him who struck them down but will truly rely on the LORD, the Holy One of Israel. A remnant will return, a remnant of Jacob will return to the Mighty God (Isa 10:20-21).

---

[181]    Ibid., 215-216.

Ezra highlights the remnant's dependence on God as they fasted and prayed prior to leaving (Ezra 8:21, 23). Additionally, in chapters 7-8, Ezra recounts the many ways in which God intervened to make their return successful. He says that the "hand" of God was upon them (7:6, 9, 28; 8:18, 22, 31).

Upon their arrival in Jerusalem, this remnant identified itself with greater Israel in their sacrificial worship. The exiles that returned "sacrificed burnt offerings to the God of Israel: twelve bulls for all Israel" (Ezra 8:35). In commenting on this verse, Joseph Blenkinsopp recalls the earlier dedication of the temple at the time of the prophets Haggai and Zechariah. He then notes the uniqueness of this later sacrifice, saying, "The difference here is the obvious concern to bring into play once again the number symbolic of the old Israel: twelve and its multiples (96 and 72). The repetition of the sin offering (*ḥaṭṭāʹt*; cf. 6:17) acknowledges that the period preceding the return was one of infidelity."[182]

About this sacrifice Mervin Breneman writes, "The first thing the returnees did was worship God. For those who love God, the first response before, during, or after any project such as this must be worship."[183]

As noted above, Ezra left Babylon with a vision of fulfilling prophecy as he returned to the land. This, however, did not fully occur. As in an earlier time when Zerubbabel and the Jews completed their work on the temple and the celebration was marked by the mixture of joy and weeping (see Ezra 3:13), so too this later return quickly fell short of prophetic expectation.

---

[182] Blenkinsopp obviously agrees with the emendation of the number 77 in the MT to 72. Joseph Blenkinsopp, *Ezra-Nehemiah* (Philadelphia: The Westminster Press, 1988), 173.

[183] Breneman, *Ezra*, 146.

In describing the response of the Jews to the completion of the temple, McConville writes,

> The joy of the people is undoubtedly portrayed as a genuine response to the exciting step forward for the community. Yet the curious mingling of joy and weeping described in v 13—such that the two sounds could not be distinguished from each other—seems to have been deliberately presented thus to suggest once again a situation that is good as far as it goes, but might be better.[184]

Ultimately, those who returned with Ezra found themselves facing a similar dilemma. Again McConville provides an important insight into Ezra's understanding of his return, stating that "Ezra depicts only a partial fulfillment, an interim situation which by its nature postulates a greater fulfillment yet to come."[185] One can only imagine how much greater fulfillment Ezra longed to see.

Within a short period of time the problem of intermarriage with the surrounding peoples surfaced. In chapters 9 and 10, the text describes Ezra confronting those who had taken foreign wives. His anguished prayer of repentance on behalf of the people is informed by his understanding of God's covenant demand for separation from all evil and spiritual compromise.

Ezra is told of this infidelity when certain leaders come to him and notify him that some of the *golah* had "mingled the holy race with the peoples around them" (9:2). The "holy race" is literally the "holy seed," *zr' hqdsh,* and is used in a metaphorical sense

---

[184] McConville, "Ezra-Nehemiah," 210.
[185] Ibid., 207.

of offspring (see Isa. 6:13). Writing about this phrase, Charles Fensham states,

> The term 'holy' shows that the term 'seed' has nothing to do with racial prejudice. It is the people whom God had elected as his people (Exod. 19:6) to carry his revelation, to be a light to the nations (Isa. 42:6) . . . . By intermingling with foreign nations and being contaminated with their idol worship, the true religion was in danger of losing its pure character.[186]

This statement underscores just how significant this remnant was perceived to be among the returnees. The spiritual and physical survival of this community was endangered. This crisis motivates Ezra to take immediate action.

Ezra responds to this news with great dismay and with an impassioned and humble prayer (Ezra 9:3-7). He repents of the sins of the people and acknowledges that God's judgment upon the nation was just (cf. Zech. 1:6). Then in verse 8, he speaks of the remnant with these words, "But now, for a brief moment, the LORD our God has been gracious in leaving us a remnant and

---

[186] Fensham, *Ezra and Nehemiah*, 125. On one level Ezra appears to see his return as related to the original Exodus. He and his fellow Jews were resettling the land and their actions can be viewed as a new conquest. On another level the "holy seed" is prophetically significant (Isa. 6:13). This "seed" serves to connect God's past plans for Israel, which failed due to Israel's spiritual infidelity, with God's future glorious plans--when Israel will finally become all that God had planned and experience all the covenant blessings that await her.

giving us a firm place in his sanctuary, and so our God gives light to our eyes and a little relief in our bondage."

He wants the remnant to recognize all that God has done for them. John Hartley notes that the word *ytd* is translated "firm place." He defines the word as "peg, stake, pin" and states, "Interestingly peg is used in a positive manner in regard to the blessing of God. Ezra speaks about the blessing God has bestowed in terms of giving a nail (RSV "secure hold") within his holy place (Ezra 9:8)."[187] This description accords with the promise of Jeremiah 31:28 where God promises to "build," *bnot*, and "plant," *nto'*, his people. These words are used in Jeremiah 24:6 to describe God's plans for the exiles.

While Jeremiah is most often remembered for his prophecies of judgment, it should also be remembered that he also preached words of return, renewal, and restoration. In referring to the words of promise in Jeremiah 24:6, J.A. Thompson writes,

> It was [Jeremiah's] great grief that the bulk of his preaching was about judgment. His references to renewal, by comparison, are few. It will be granted to the exiles to know Yahweh and to form the nucleus of the renewed Israel which will recognize Yahweh's sovereignty. They will *return* (*šûb*) to him with their whole heart. Heart renewal could evidently come only after judgment, so that judgment was the very means by which the new beginning for God's people was to be achieved—an encouraging doctrine for those in exile and for those who would follow in 586 B.C.[188]

---

[187]  John E. Hartley, "יתד," *TWOT*, 1:418-419.
[188]  Thompson, *Jeremiah*, 508.

The words of Ezra's prayer are particularly instructive in relation to understanding both his character and his theology. This prayer also provides insight into his personal struggle. Writing about this prayer, the commentators Allen and Laniak state,

> The narrator presents the postexilic period with deliberate ambivalence. It had a negative side. The shock waves of foreign invasions and the fall of Jerusalem continued to reverberate in the community's present experience (**as it is today**, v.7). Political independence **(our kings)** had given way to the control of **foreign kings**, which meant political and economic **bondage** . . . . Yet the storm clouds had a silver lining in postexilic experience. The long period of deserved oppression at the hands of Assyrian and Babylonian **kings** had been succeeded by a comparatively **brief moment** of God's surprising grace in the postexilic era. Evidence of a **new** lease on **life** lay all around Ezra and the bystanders as they stood in the grounds of the rebuilt temple, which was a symbol of their firm "foothold" (REB) in the land. God's grace, providentially mediated through the Persian empire, had restored them from exile as a **remnant** surviving judgment (bold in text).[189]

Ezra was certainly aware of the negatives in relation to the remnant's present condition, but as Allen and Laniak point out, they had also experienced repatriation in the context of God's favor. Ezra understood this and gave thanks.

---

[189] L. Allen and T. Laniak, *Ezra, Nehemiah, Esther* (Peabody, MA: Hendrickson, 2003), 76.

As was discussed earlier, the remnant theme plays a key role both in the exile and in the return. Writing about this idea, Mervin Breneman states,

> The term "remnant" is significant in the theology of the prophets, such as Isaiah, Jeremiah, and Zechariah. The prophets lost hope in political Israel for the future of God's kingdom. They prophesied that God would continue his plan through a "remnant." . . . Ezra knew how important this "remnant" was for God's plan. Only a pure and separate "remnant" would be useful to God in his plan of redemption, which was to provide the Scriptures and the Savior for all the world. This helps explain Ezra's seemingly "radical" policies.[190]

In his prayer, Ezra served as the spokesman for this remnant as he expressed words of repentance. Significantly, Ezra did not stand alone in his grief over the infidelity of some. The text says, "Then everyone who trembled at the words of the God of Israel gathered around me because of the unfaithfulness of the exiles" (Ezra 9:4). Whereas the preexilic prophets were so often forced to stand alone, Ezra experienced support by a group of unnamed Jews. Again Breneman provides an important insight:

> The phrase "everyone who trembled at the words of God" was used, especially in the postexilic community, of those who strictly observed the law. It denotes an attitude of openness to what God says and a readiness to obey. A number of people were concerned about

---

[190]  Breneman, *Ezra*, 153.

the problem and began gathering around Ezra. They needed a leader to express the problem and take the necessary initiative. We might think that Ezra was overly dramatic, but the response shows the attractiveness of holy zeal . . . . Those who tremble at the Word of God will tremble at human sin. Today's spirit of acceptance and broad-mindedness has much to learn from Ezra's "immoderate godliness."[191]

Another important insight relating to Ezra's prayer as it connects to the Jeremiah 31 passage is found in Ezra's repentance. In Jeremiah the words of repentance come from the mouth of Ephraim (v.18). The link between the two passages, Ezra 9 and Jeremiah 31, is seen in v.19 of Jeremiah and v.6 of Ezra 9. In Jeremiah, Ephraim says that after he strayed, he repented and beat his breast. He adds, "I was ashamed and humiliated," *bshti vgm-nklmti*, bearing the disgrace of his youth. In Ezra 9:6, Ezra prays to God saying, "I am too ashamed and disgraced" *bshti vnklmti*, "to lift up my face to you, my God, because our sins are higher than our heads and our guilt has reached to the heavens." In his analysis of these two texts McConville notes,

The verbal allusion in this case is noteworthy because of the compound expression. And the correspondence of theme is equally interesting because Jer. xxxi is the most explicit among the prophetic texts relating to restoration in making repentance (here in the mouth of Ephraim)

---

[191]  Ibid., 150-151. Here Ezra demonstrates a reverent fear of God. This attitude serves to maintain the distinction between clean and unclean (see previous discussion).

an immediate ground of that restoration. The appeal of this element in Jer. xxxi to our author in Ezra is that it affords a point of contact in a prophetic text relating to restoration for the exiles' situation, which is claimed to fulfill prophecy, yet which is still characterized by sin and which therefore demands repentance. Both texts hold together the ideas of repentance and of God's salvation. Ezra uses the collocation in Jer xxxi to resolve the tension of the exiles' situation in which the objects of the saving act still sin . . . . Ezra's act of repentance, therefore (ix 3-4), is part of the act of salvation. The effect of it—in terms of applying prophecy to Ezra's time—is to suggest that that act is in the process of happening, rather than that it has happened once and for all.[192]

While Ezra may have lived with a certain tension as to how the prophetic promises concerning the restoration of Judah and Israel would ultimately be fulfilled, there seems little doubt that he believed that his return had prophetic value. In relation to Ezra's prayer, McConville makes this summary statement: "It follows from our study so far that the prayer of Ezra uses motifs from both Jer. xxxi and Isa. xl-lxvi, in ways that are both overlapping and complementary, in order to express the belief that the exiles' situation is a stage on the way to an ultimate fulfillment of prophecy."[193] This is truly a remarkable statement.

Ezra's words reflect his understanding of God's goodness and mercy extended to Israel in the context of living under Persian

---

[192]  McConville, "Ezra-Nehemiah," 216-217.

[193]  Ibid., 222.

rule (9:9). On the one hand, these Jews longed for complete restoration and independence since they lived "as slaves," to quote Ezra. However, Ezra recognizes that God has not "deserted" or "abandoned," *'zb*, his people. This same word, *'zb*, was used to describe Israel's condition in exile. Speaking through the prophet Isaiah, God spoke of having temporarily "abandoned," *'zb*, his people (54:7). He spoke of them having been abandoned in a manner similar to that of a wife being abandoned by her husband (see Isa. 54:6; 60:15; 62:4).

In Ezra, however, the text demonstrates that Israel was not abandoned by God. He faithfully cared for them. Ezra continues by saying that they had experienced God's "kindness," *hsd,* "in the sight of the kings of Persia" (9:9). This word, *hsd,* is a strongly relational word. D. A. Baer and R. P. Gordon describe several important aspects of divine *hsd.* They state,

> Divine חֶסֶד saves people from disaster or oppressors. The biblical writers seem persuaded that life is fragile. One lives surrounded by the threat posed by the calamities of nature, the hostility of enemies, and the weakness of self. These same writers plead for God to save them by his חֶסֶד, and they recognize that this effective loyalty on God's part is their only hedge against disaster . . . .

> Divine חֶסֶד sustains life. The dynamic power of death is near at hand in the experience of the OT writers. It is an invading power that seeks every opportunity to drag one down and cut off one's life. God's חֶסֶד counteracts this power. It is an ally of life, a hedge against the threatening power of death . . . .

Divine חֶסֶד counteracts God's wrath. At times the biblical text suggests that God's *own* response to human sin runs in opposite directions. At such moments, God's חֶסֶד exercises an ameliorating or limiting role upon his wrath . . . .

Divine חֶסֶד is enduring, persistent, even eternal. The biblical writers celebrate the everlastingness of God's חֶסֶד . . . .

Divine חֶסֶד is regarded as the basis or motive for petition or approach to God. Sinners seek forgiveness on the basis of God's חֶסֶד . . . .

Divine חֶסֶד occupies a prominent role in the inner and communal life of God's people.[194]

Not only has Israel not been abandoned, the people have in fact experienced God's kindness, and more than that, God has granted them "new life," *mhyh*. This word is derived from the verb *hyh*. Here Ezra uses this prophetically significant word. Terry Brensinger defines *hyh* as "be alive, be revived, come back to life." He describes its use in the latter prophets,

Ezekiel compares the nation to a valley of dry and parched bones that return to life (Ezek 37:1-14). Of theological significance here is the fact that this act of reviving dry bones occurs through the proclamation of the word of Yahweh, as well as through the receiving of his Spirit. Furthermore, being restored to life results in Israel's returning to the land and knowing that Yahweh is the Lord.

---

[194]  D. A. Baer and R. P. Gordon, "חסד," *NIDOTTE* 2:213-16.

As such, Yahweh's life-giving activities are not simply ends in themselves; they are, in fact, acts of revelation.[195]

From Ezra's perspective, this new life began with the earlier return that led to the rebuilding of the temple and restoring of the ruins. This last phrase, *'t-hrbtin vlh'mid*, "and to repair its ruins" (Ezra 9:9) points to the reversal of Yahweh's earlier action in "laying waste" the land (see Jer. 7:34; 25:11).

Finally, this verse provides remarkable insight into Ezra's theological understanding. He says that God gave the *golah* "a wall," *gdr*, of protection in Judah and Jerusalem. The word *gdr* is used in the Bible in both its literal and figurative sense. In Ezekiel 13 God condemns the false prophets, saying,

Woe to the foolish prophets who follow their own spirit and have seen nothing! Your prophets, O Israel, are like jackals among ruins. You have not gone up to the breaks in the wall to repair it for the house of Israel so that it will stand firm in the battle on the day of the Lord. Their visions are false and their divinations a lie (13:3-6a).

In this passage the wall is used figuratively to point to the spiritual deficiencies that existed among God's people. One role of a prophet was to alert the people to the dangers that lay ahead if they continued to stray. They were to warn and admonish God's people. These earlier prophets, however, were unconcerned for the spiritual well-being of the people. They lived simply to benefit themselves (see also Hosea 2:6).

---

195  Terry L. Brensinger, "חיה," *NIDOTTE*, 2:110.

In Ezra 9, is Ezra speaking of the wall in a literal or figurative sense? Depending on when Ezra prayed these words, it may have been that Nehemiah had already completed the wall. However, it seems more likely that Ezra is using the word in its figurative sense. This is supported by the fact that he says that this wall of protection covers Judah and Jerusalem. There definitely was no literal wall around all of Judah. Also, from the rest of the prayer it seems unlikely that he is referring to the Persian presence as a wall of protection, as advanced by Blenkinsopp.[196] Rather, as Breneman states, "Ezra here was not talking about the Jerusalem wall but about God's protection for the Jewish community."[197]

Finally, writing about Ezra's prayer, A. Philip Brown comments, "Ezra's prayer, reflecting his skill in the Law, penetrated to the heart of the principle Yahweh established in the Law, namely, the fact that any alliance that endangers or compromises wholehearted devotion to Yahweh is forbidden."[198]

Next, in chapter 10 one observes the *golah*, led by Shecaniah, coming to Ezra with these words,

We have been unfaithful to our God by marrying foreign women from the peoples around us. But in spite of this, there is still hope for Israel. Now let us make a covenant before our God to send away all these women and their children, in accordance with the counsel of my lord and of those who fear the commands of our God (vv. 2-3).

---

[196] Blenkinsopp, *Ezra-Nehemiah*, 184.

[197] Breneman, *Ezra*, 153-154.

[198] A. Philip Brown II, "The Problem of Mixed Marriages in Ezra 9-10," *BSac* 162 (October-December 2005): 451.

In reading the words of Shecaniah, one notes that he joined Ezra in repenting before God for the sins of the people. He recognized the sin that the people had committed (i.e., they had married foreign women). One can only wonder, however, about his words of hope that follow. He says that "there is still hope for Israel" (v.2b). With these words, was he downplaying the sin of the people? Or was he seeing something that is not immediately recognizable from the text? Commenting on the words of Shecaniah, Fredrick Holmgren writes,

> A representative of this group, Shecaniah, confesses the faithlessness of the community that is reflected in the marriage of Jewish men with "foreign women" (v.2). Despite the seriousness of the sin, however, Shecaniah is convinced that the community can avoid judgment if the people pledge to God (i.e., "make a covenant" with God) that they will "put away" (lit. "bring out"; cf. v. 19 and Deut. 24:1-2) the foreign wives and their children. On behalf of the community, Shecaniah calls upon Ezra to take the lead in initiating this new action (v. 4).[199]

Shecaniah was not excusing the sin. Rather, he believed that the community was capable of responding appropriately to this crisis (i.e., with repentance). Fensham's logic is as follows: "All is not lost; there is still hope for Israel. The logical outcome from the prayer of Ezra is that if the iniquity is removed, there would be forgiveness for their sin. God is righteous: he is a God of grace.

---

[199] Fredrick C. Holmgren, *Ezra & Nehemiah: Israel Alive Again* (Grand Rapids: Eerdmans, 1987), 80.

Thus there is hope."[200] Shecaniah's theology appears to be built around the closely linked ideas of repentance and restoration. If God's people do not stay in their sin, but take the initiative to repent and return to following the commands of God, then he will not have to judge them. Shecaniah understood something of the grace, faithfulness, and covenant love of God.

Ezra responded by putting the spiritual leaders, the leading priests and Levites, and all Israel under oath to do what Shecaniah had requested. Then, Ezra withdrew and continued to fast and pray. Next, all the *golah* were called to Jerusalem under threat of being expelled from the assembly (v.8).

The urgency of the situation is underscored by the fact that Ezra confronted the people as they stood in the temple square in the rain (v.9). Ezra accused the people of "spiritual infidelity," *m'l*, to God. This was the same accusation that God lodged against Israel in the past (see Ezek. 20:27).

That this accusation resonated with the people is evident from v.12: "The whole assembly responded with a loud voice: 'You are right! We must do as you say.'" What follows is a request for time and for the local officials to be allowed to investigate each case. Do their words make sense? Yes. Fensham provides three arguments from v.13 for allowing the leaders to decide the individual cases. He says,

First, the people gathered there were a large crowd, and it would take a long time to organize the crowd. Second, it was raining and they were standing in the open without protection. The situation was not favorable for a calm investigation; tempers could flare up easily . . . . Third,

---

[200] Fensham, *Ezra and Nehemiah*, 134.

a great number of cases had to be decided. Some of them might be problematical. It was thus unwise to draw hasty conclusions and to commit an injustice to people.[201]

That there was strong agreement to this proposal is evident by that fact that only four people are listed as opposing this plan. The book ends with a three-month investigation, followed by action taken against those found guilty of this act of infidelity. Writing about the actions taken here by Ezra and the Jewish community, Mark Throntveit says, "It is not their racial or national ties that are at issue but the religious practices that the foreign wives brought to their marriages and the effects those practices would surely have had upon family and community structures."[202] One needs only remember the negative impact that a wife like Jezebel had on Israel.

A. Philip Brown summarizes the mixed marriage crisis emphasizing the importance of holiness:

Perhaps the most obvious implication of the [marriage] crisis is the supreme importance of holiness. Holiness was absolutely essential for the continuation and well-being of the returnees . . . .

A second implication is that holiness is more important than even the closest of human relationships: marriage. Although divorce is hateful to God, this episode reinforces the principle taught in Deuteronomy 13 that unswerving

---

[201]   Ibid., 140.

[202]   Mark A. Throntveit, *Ezra-Nehemiah* (Louisville: John Knox Press, 1992), 57.

loyalty to Yahweh is of far greater importance than the continuance of marriage . . . .

For Israel holiness was therefore not primarily a matter of how one behaved within the sacred precincts of the temple, but how one lived in every area of his or her life . . . . The holiness or unholiness of each person affected the entire community's standing before God. What 113 men had done brought the entire community under His wrath (Ezra 10:14).[203]

In summary, Ezra understood the return under Sheshbazzar and later his own return as both divinely motivated and the fulfillment of earlier prophecy. He recognized that repentance leads to restoration, and that a life lived in obedience to Torah was pleasing to Yahweh and would result in joy and blessing. At the same time, he seemed to know that his return resulted in only a partial fulfillment of prophecy, and that greater fulfillment was yet to come.

## Prophetic Fulfillment in Nehemiah

Both Ezra and Nehemiah went up to Jerusalem during roughly the same time period, seeking the well-being of the city and its citizens. However, their backgrounds, their specific goals, and their methods were quite different. Ezra, a priest, is described as "a teacher well versed in the Law of Moses" (7:6), who "had devoted himself to the study and observance of the Law of the

---

[203] Brown, "The Problem of Mixed Marriages," 458.

Lord and to teaching its decrees and laws in Israel" (7:10). Ezra went to Jerusalem as a teacher and spiritual leader.

Nehemiah, who also knew the laws and decrees of Moses (see Neh. 1:7-9), traveled to Jerusalem, not as a priest or teacher, but as a loyal subject of the Persian king. His mission was to "promote the welfare of the Israelites," (2:10) specifically those living in and around Jerusalem.

Hugh Williamson describes three features of Nehemiah's life and ministry. The first is Nehemiah's "unsophisticated manner [of describing] previous national history . . . . For a lay person, a simple reference to a well-known story is more effective, for being more readily intelligible, than legalistic niceties."[204] The second feature is Nehemiah's uncomplicated approach to religion. For Nehemiah, things were generally black or white. As an example, Nehemiah rebuffs the devious Shemaiah's attempt to lure him into the sanctuary with the simple words, "Should a man in my position run away? Or who in my state would enter the temple and live?" (Neh. 6:11)[205] The third feature is Nehemiah's lay approach to the institutions of religion. Here, too, his attitude was clear and simple. For example, God had commanded the observance of the Sabbath, and the Jerusalem community was not obeying God's command. Therefore, Nehemiah took strong, measured steps to provide the necessary conditions for Sabbath observation (see Neh. 13:15-21).[206] Nehemiah was a humble man of action who maintained a simple and practical faith in God. Nehemiah's life and faith were typical of that of a lay person. He believed that if

---

[204] Hugh G. M. Williamson, "The Belief System of the Book of Nehemiah," in *The Crisis of Israelite Religion* (Leiden: Brill, 1999), 278.

[205] Ibid., 279, 280.

[206] Ibid., 280.

God gave a command to his people, then they were required to obey it.

The Book of Nehemiah comments on the response of God's people to the positive and negative challenges of life. Their responses provide important insight into the spiritual condition of the *golah* during this part of the Persian era.

In chapter 1, Nehemiah's mission was conceived and developed following the reception of a report from a brother, Hanani, who described conditions in Jerusalem. He reported to Nehemiah, "Those who survived the exile and are back in the province are in great trouble and disgrace. The wall of Jerusalem is broken down, and its gates have been burned with fire" (1:3). This news marked a turning point in Nehemiah's life that led him to prayer and then to Jerusalem, where he organized the rebuilding of the wall around the city. This became a milestone event in relation to the spiritual well-being of the Jews in Jerusalem.

Several experiences preceded the rebuilding of the wall. Two of these will be listed. First, there was the repentance that took place in Babylon (Zech. 1:6). This set the stage for the return that resulted from Cyrus's decree (Ezra 1:1-4). The second major event was the rebuilding of the temple. As noted above, God used the prophets Haggai and Zechariah to motivate the *golah* to action. He also worked through the words and deeds of Persian kings (see Ezra 6:13-15).

These two events preceded the rebuilding of the wall. To accomplish this later task, God placed a burden on the heart of Nehemiah, who planned and organized the rebuilding of the wall. Nehemiah understood the strategic importance of the wall to the physical and spiritual well-being of the Jewish community in Jerusalem. Writing about the wall, M. D. Goulder states,

Nehemiah 6 marks the breakthrough of his enterprise. Several plots to murder Nehemiah are frustrated, and the wall is completed: 'and when all our enemies heard of it, all the nations round about saw, and fell greatly in their own esteem: for they perceived that this had been accomplished with the help of our God' (6.16). We hear the same note in Psalm 126: 'When the LORD restored the fortunes of Zion, we were like those who dream. Then our mouth was filled with laughter, and our tongue with shouts of joy; then it was said among the nations, The LORD has done great things for them. The LORD has done great things for us, and we rejoice' (vv. 1-3). With Nehemiah's coming the Exile is substantially over. Israel is (quasi-) independent once more; and the Sanballat's and Geshem's, and all the peoples around, have recognized the decisive action of Yahweh. The joy rings clear across two and a half millennia. There is still more restoration ahead, which the LORD will perform as he floods the wadis in the Negev. Those who left Jerusalem in 587 sowed in tears, but in 445 their descendants reap in joy.[207]

It would be hard to overstate the significance of this event. But what evidence exists in the Book of Nehemiah for the claim that prophecy was being fulfilled and that the *golah* experienced spiritual renewal? In what ways were the postexilic Jews significantly different from their preexilic ancestors?

It is evident that Nehemiah's mission was rooted in prayer based on genuine faith. Several aspects of this prayer stand out

---

[207] M. D. Goulder, "The Songs of Ascents and Nehemiah," *JSOT* 75 (1997): 51.

(chapter 1 ff.). These include Nehemiah's knowledge of the person and character of God, his attentiveness to the need of confession/repentance, his understanding of the words and promises of God, and his insight into how to petition God. These aspects of his prayer draw attention to the fact that Nehemiah had received careful biblical instruction and that he applied what he learned to his life. Breneman identifies this as a prayer of repentance. He says, "It can be outlined as follows: (a) invocation to God; (b) confession of sins; (c) request to the LORD to remember his people; (d) request for success."[208]

First, the prayer points to his knowledge of God (v.5). He knew God as Yahweh, the God of heaven, the God who is great and awesome,[209] and the God who faithfully keeps covenant love with his people. This invocation expresses the greatness and fearsomeness of God, but it also includes aspects of his mercy and covenant love. Breneman examines Nehemiah's prayer:

'The great and awesome God' indicates Nehemiah's appreciation of who God is: the one whom Nehemiah feared and the source and object of his deep faith. God's awesomeness is the impression his total character and person leaves on all who encounter him . . . .

---

[208] Breneman, *Ezra*, 171.

[209] This combination, "great and awesome," is used ten times in the OT, three times in Nehemiah (9:32 adds "mighty"). Nehemiah's usage of this phrase appears to draw directly from Deut. 7:21 where Moses instructs the people not to be terrified by the nations living in the land because God, who is "great and awesome," will drive them out.

One central theme of the Old Testament is God's special covenant relation with his people. The word *ḥesed* (translated here "love" in "covenant of love") is used frequently in the Old Testament. It is closely related to the covenant and contains the idea of loyalty.[210]

Second, Nehemiah confessed the sins of Israel, his family sins, and his personal disobedience to the commands of God (vv.6-7). He uses the word "confess," *mtodh*, in its Hithpael participle form. Ralph Alexander states,

> The Hithpael form is normally employed when this verb is used to convey the confession of national sins. This stem was also employed when the great confessions of Israel's were made by Daniel (9:4, 20), Ezra (10:1), Nehemiah (1:6), and the people of Israel (9:2-3) during and after the Babylonian captivity.[211]

His words of confession demonstrate an understanding of the seriousness of Israel's past sin and rebellion. Words such as these support the central thesis of this paper that Israel experienced national repentance during its exile in Babylon, without which the return and all that followed would have been impossible.

Next, Nehemiah reminds God of his words and promises (1:8-9). This is followed by Nehemiah's request. About these words Mark Throntveit writes,

---

[210] Ibid.

[211] Ralph H. Alexander, "ידה," *TWOT*, 1:364. The most well-known example of personal confession of sin comes from the life and words of King David (see Ps 32:5; 51:1-4).

The heart of the prayer is also its turning point (vv. 8-9). Nehemiah reminds God that the lesson has been learned; the exiles have been scattered among the peoples for their unfaithfulness. This is to be seen as a testimony to God's power and control of history. Israel is in God's hands, not subject to the capricious machinations of human despots. Therefore, God's judgment upon Israel's sin, related in the summary of Deuteronomy 30:1-5 in Nehemiah 1:8, has been carried out. But as the positive confession of verse 10 intimates ("your servants") and verse 11a declares ("your servants who delight in revering your name"), the signs of repentance are present as well, and so Nehemiah appeals to God to remember the promise of return also contained in Deuteronomy 30:1-5 (1:9).[212]

Throntveit sees signs of Israel's repentance and transformation in Nehemiah's confession of sin and also in the reverential attitude exhibited both by Nehemiah and by others of the remnant. This attitude is expressed in the words, "who delight in revering your name," *hhptsim lir'h 't-shmk*. The word "delight," *hpts*, used here as a verbal adjective, is defined by David Talley as "(1) having delight or pleasure about s.t.; having longing or desire for s.t.; (2) willing."[213] The attitude communicated in these words contrasts with the attitude of the people in preexilic Judah. For example, through Jeremiah God said, "To whom can I speak and give warning? Who will listen to me? Their ears are closed so they cannot hear. The word of the LORD is offensive to them; they find no *pleasure* in

---

[212] Throntveit, *Ezra-Nehemiah*, 65.

[213] David Talley, "חפץ," *NIDOTTE*, 2:231.

it" (italics added; Jer. 6:10). There was no interest in hearing or, much less, obeying the words of God.

Next, as Nehemiah and the *golah* take up the work of rebuilding the wall, the attitude and commitment of these people stand out. In chapter 4 one finds the people working "with all their heart" (v.6) and petitioning God when threatened (v.9). In his discussion of their work on the wall, Breneman states, "'So we rebuilt the wall' is a commendation of God's faithfulness in response to prayer and of the people's courage and determination. The people continued steadfastly toward the goal even in the face of ridicule. The faith, unity, and energy of the small group prevailed."[214]

## Community Issues

In chapter 5, Nehemiah was forced to intervene in the internal problems that developed within the Jewish community. Injustice, oppressive conditions, and taxes led to food shortages and to families losing their land and being forced to sell their children into slavery. It appears, also, that "loan sharks" seized an opportunity for profiteering. How was this situation resolved?

In some ways, these conditions recall the situation in Jeremiah 34. There Jerusalem was under siege by the Chaldean army. During an earlier time Zedekiah "made a covenant with all the people in Jerusalem to proclaim freedom for the slaves" (v.8). Everyone was to free his male and female Hebrew slaves. Unfortunately, the text continues, "But afterward they changed their minds and took back the slaves they had freed and enslaved them again" (v.11).

----

[214] Breneman, *Ezra*, 195.

This action was condemned by God (v.16). When the pressure was removed, the people reverted to their previous ways.

In Nehemiah 5, Nehemiah condemned the nobles and officials for exacting usury from their countrymen (v.7). He told them to give back what they had taken, to which the leaders agreed (v.12). Nehemiah then put these leaders under oath, and in a symbolic act, shook out the folds of his robe (v.13a). What is remarkable is the response of the whole assembly (13b). They said, "'Amen,' and praised the LORD. And the people did as they had promised." Writing about this verse Charles Fensham notes,

> In v.13 a symbolic act of Nehemiah is described. In those days people kept some of their personal belongings in the folds of their gowns or garments. We may call it the pocket of the gown. Nehemiah emptied the pocket before the people, shaking out everything. This became now a symbol of a curse, a kind of rite he performed to illustrate the curse. It was shown to the people in its empty state to signify that, if they should fail to keep the promise, they would be shaken out in the same manner and they would have nothing left . . . . Nehemiah's drastic measures were thus successful. It is obvious that Nehemiah and Ezra followed different courses with the people. Nehemiah, with the authority of a governor, could accuse the guilty, convict them, and consequently take penal measures. He acted on his own. Ezra, on the contrary, left the decisions to the leaders and then acted on what they had decided.[215]

---

[215]  Fensham, *Ezra and Nehemiah*, 197.

The outcome in Nehemiah was very different from what occurred in Jeremiah 34. Breneman states that "the unselfish leadership and courageous action of Nehemiah bore fruit: not only did the offenders do as they had promised, but they also restored unity and praised the Lord."[216]

Turning next to Nehemiah 8, one finds Ezra reading the Book of the Law of Moses to all the people (v.1). On the first day of the seventh month, the day marking the Feast of Trumpets (see Lev. 23:24), the people observed a sacred assembly. Several notable details about this assembly are included in the text. First, all the people listened "attentively" as Ezra read (v.3). Second, when Ezra opened the book, the people responded by standing up (v.5). Here, Breneman notes, "Standing in reverence and acceptance of God's authority in the Scripture must have been customary. In Neh. 9:3 we note the same tradition of standing for reading the Torah, for confession of sin, and for worship."[217]

Third, when Ezra praised the LORD (v.6), the people lifted their hands and replied with "Amen, Amen," and then bowed with faces to the ground and worshiped the LORD. Fourth, as the text was read and explained, the people reacted with mourning and weeping (v.9). This response reflected a sensitivity to God's Word along with a spirit of repentance as the people recognized their sin and their failure to keep the requirements of the Law.

Fifth, the element of joy permeates the rest of the chapter beginning with v.10. However, as noted above, the initial response of the people was not with joy. They were grieved. It took Ezra, Nehemiah and the Levites to get the people calmed down. Nehemiah tells the people not to grieve with the famous phrase,

------

[216]   Breneman, *Ezra*, 206.

[217]   Ibid., 225

"for the joy of the LORD is your strength," *ki-hdot yhovh hi' m'zzkm*. Michael Grisanti states that the word joy, *hdh*, describes "God's nature as one of joy and strength (1 Chron. 16:27; Neh. 8:10)."[218]

In his commentary, Fredrick Holmgren states that joy was part of Israel's experience with Yahweh from the beginning of its nationhood. He writes,

> Rejoicing in the God who brought them out of the 'iron furnace' (Deut. 4:20) reminds them of the hope they have in the most distressing situations. Further, remembering Yahweh and rejoicing in him gives Israel strength to say yes to his way of life and no to those paths that lead to oppression and ruin.[219]

Additionally, joy was part of the prophetic promise of Jeremiah 31. Verse 13b says, "I will turn their mourning into gladness; I will give them comfort and joy instead of sorrow." Yahweh promised that joy would be part of Israel's future experience as he acted to "redeem them from the hand of those stronger than they" (Jer. 31:11).

Breneman provides what may be an underlying element at work in chapter 8 by noting that what occurs here is typical of a "synagogue service: (1) the assembly of the people; (2) the request for reading of the Torah; (3) the opening of the scroll; (4) the people standing; (5) the praise (by Ezra); (6) the response of the people; (7) sermon instruction; (8) reading the law; (9) oral explanation and exhortation; (10) departure

---

[218]   Michael Grisanti, "חדה," *NIDOTTE*, 2:25.

[219]   Holmgren, *Israel Alive Again*, 126.

for a fellowship meal (v.10)."[220] He continues, "It is significant that this reading of the law and the worship service were not centered in the temple and not controlled by the priesthood. From this time on in Judaism, the Torah was more important than the temple."[221]

This statement leads to the following question: In what ways, if any, did the temple function differently at the time of Ezra and Nehemiah than it had during the preexilic era?

One could argue that in many ways the temple continued to function as it had in earlier times. For example, for large gatherings, for the offering of sacrifices, for the collection of tithes and offerings, and as the main center of religious activity, the temple existed as the single most important place in Judaism. Writing in *The Crisis of Israelite Religion*, Bob Becking notes, "[T]he temple was very important for the religious identity of postexilic Judaism. The temple gave them a home to gather and to worship YHWH in a world where other religions and other forms of Yahwism were present."[222] The temple and the temple mount along with the historic significance of Jerusalem served as a powerful unifying force within Second Temple Judaism.

However, with the new emphasis given to religious instruction, centered on the reading and application of Torah, it seems reasonable to conclude that the temple took on a new

---

[220] Breneman, *Ezra*, 224.

[221] Ibid. This is an interesting observation, though it is noteworthy that Ezra was a priest. Did his actions in chapter 8 reflect worship in Babylon?

[222] Bob Becking, "Continuity and Community: The Belief System of the Book of Ezra," in *The Crisis of Israelite Religion*, ed. Bob Becking and Marjo C.A. Korpel (Leiden: Brill, 1999), 269.

function: it became the central location of instruction for the covenant community. There the Torah and the other inspired writings assumed a uniquely prominent place in sustaining the essential beliefs and practices of Judaism. Consequently, the temple became the major gathering place both for rabbis and for the faithful seeking instruction. Further, according to Ezekiel 37:1-14, Israel owed its very life to the resurrecting power of the Spirit of God. Consequently, emergent Second Temple Judaism (i.e. Judaism of the early Persian Period) was founded on Word and Spirit.[223]

Finally, it seems significant that Sabbath and Sabbath-keeping, while not mentioned in the Book of Ezra, are mentioned nine times in Nehemiah. Ezra, as a priest, had enormous concern for the temple. In the first chapters of the book, Ezra traces the rebuilding of the temple. In chapter 7, Ezra's concern shifts. He travels from Babylon to Jerusalem carrying a large amount of silver and gold along with sacred articles. Upon arrival in Jerusalem, Ezra goes to great pains to account for all that has been entrusted to him. His concern is that the temple be a place where God is honored (7:27; 8:33-34). On the other hand, Nehemiah's concern for the temple appears to have been primarily related to its function, as the place where offerings were collected and religious activities took place. Consequently, he wanted to see the temple well maintained and also free from reproach (see 11:16; 13:4-14).

Once the wall was completed, Nehemiah's concern shifted. With the external/foreign forces controlled, the people could live in obedience to Torah (10:28-39). Of particular concern to him

---

[223] The spiritual dimension of their lives undergirds all the activities of Ezra and Nehemiah. Both were men of Word and Spirit.

was the fact that Sabbath-keeping had been abandoned both in and around Jerusalem. Fensham observes,

> The Sabbath law was totally forgotten. The real meaning of the Sabbath, a day to acknowledge the Lord as Creator and to give all the honor to him for a successful week, had been abandoned. The Sabbath was celebrated to show that man's existence as a creation was more important than his fight for survival. It is one of the significant phenomena which distinguished the Jews from other nations.[224]

Consequently, Nehemiah took deliberate steps to provide for Sabbath-keeping and to bring about the conditions wherein God's people could return to their weekly worship of Yahweh.

Finally, both Ezra and Nehemiah must have wondered about Israel's future. Both men met with a measure of success in their ministries among the *golah*. Within this community there existed a sensitivity to sin and a recognition of responsibility to live within the covenant. Consequently, when Ezra confronted the *golah* about their unfaithfulness to Yahweh by marrying foreign/pagan women, these people responded with contrition and obedience to Ezra's instruction (Ezra 10:12-17). Nehemiah witnessed the response of God's people both in the rebuilding of the wall and in the setting up of the physical and spiritual structures so that the Sabbath and the other religious ordinances could be properly observed.

---

[224]  Fensham, *Ezra and Nehemiah*, 263-64.

## Summary

An important question asked in this study is this: Did God fulfill the promise recorded in Jeremiah 24:4-7 as it pertains to the Jewish exiles taken to Babylon? Verse 7 ends with the words: "for they will return to me with all their heart." Was a new relationship between God and his people established during Israel's time in Babylon? If so, then one would expect to find evidence pointing to this new relationship in the postexilic writings.

In chapters 3 and 4 two postexilic eras were examined, the first in Haggai and Zechariah 1-8 and the second in Ezra and Nehemiah. During the first period the temple was rebuilt. Three important themes emerged from the Haggai/Zechariah study: the themes of reversal, of divine sovereignty, and of a new world order. The theme of reversal was particularly important, for during the ministries of Jeremiah and Ezekiel God's judgment, as described in the covenant curses, loomed over Judah (Jer. 19:1-13). In the early postexilic era, however, as the people began to rebuild, God returned his blessing to the people and the land (Hag. 2:19). In Zechariah 8:12 this same promise is repeated. Both passages allude to the promise found in Ezekiel 34:27, the promise of renewed fertility. The idea of reversal can also be seen in God's promise to "do good again to Jerusalem and Judah" (Zech. 8:15): the *golah* experienced God's favor. Another example of reversal is found in relation to the fasts that had been observed during the time of captivity. While the fasts had previously been times of sorrow and grief, God transformed them into times of joy (see Zech. 8:19).

These reversals illustrate God's response to the repentant and obedient spirit that existed among the *golah*. God sovereignly worked among this remnant and began to establish a new world order. This new world order began in the postexilic era and at the same time anticipated greater fulfillment in the future with the coming of God's servant, the Branch (Zech. 3:8).

Many of the themes found in Haggai and Zechariah 1-8 are also found in Ezra and Nehemiah. With Ezra bringing back the gold, silver, and the sacred items to the temple, a major reversal occurred. As recorded in Ezra 2 and 3, those who returned gave freely to the rebuilding of the temple. It is also recorded that in the seventh month "the people assembled as one man in Jerusalem" (Ezra 3:1). There existed a spirit of unity among the remnant. These actions reflect fulfillment of Jeremiah 24:7.

A new belief system appears to have been established in Babylon, built on the twin pillars of repentance and Torah. These two pillars played a major role in the life of the community and its leaders as they reestablished themselves in Jerusalem and rebuilt the wall. The prayers of Ezra and Nehemiah reflect their knowledge of Torah and also their recognition of the essential nature of repentance (see Ezra 10 and Nehemiah 1). They understood that repentance leads to restoration.

The construction of the wall around Jerusalem stands out as a milestone event in the biblical record. A truly remarkable trait exhibited by the builders was their faith, unity, and determination in completing the task. Additionally, when the leaders were confronted with their ungodly behavior (Nehemiah 5), they responded properly to the rebuke. While sin continued to be a problem, the *golah* exhibited sensitivity to the word of God that was lacking in the preexilic era.

# CHAPTER 5

# THE EARLY PERSIAN PERIOD AND THE ARCHAEOLOGICAL RECORD

Jeremiah's prophecy concerning Judah's time of exile in Babylon appears to have been in the forefront of the thinking of many of the Jews living in captivity. For example, Daniel 9:2 says, "In the first year of his [King Darius's] reign, I, Daniel, understood from the Scriptures, according to the word of the Lord given to Jeremiah the prophet, that the desolation of Jerusalem would last seventy years." Realizing that the seventy years were at or nearing completion, Daniel fasted and prayed, confessing the sins of the nation and petitioning God for mercy both on his people and on Jerusalem (9:4-19).

In the final chapter of the Book of Chronicles, after the description of Nebuchadnezzar's conquest of Jerusalem and his exiling of the Jews to Babylon, the text states, "The land enjoyed its sabbath rests; all the time of its desolation it rested, until the seventy years were completed in fulfillment of the word of the Lord spoken by Jeremiah" (2 Chron. 36:21). The Book of Ezra begins with these words, "In the first year of Cyrus king of Persia, in order to fulfill the word of the Lord spoken by Jeremiah, the Lord moved the heart of Cyrus king of Persia to make a proclamation . . ." (Ezra 1:1). Even the "angel of the Lord" in Zechariah expressed concern over the years that had lapsed on the prophetic calendar. The angel said, "Lord Almighty, how long will you withhold mercy from Jerusalem and from the towns of Judah, which you have been angry with these seventy years?" (Zech. 1:12; see also Zech. 7:5). From these examples, it is clear that during Judah's time in Babylon the exiles watched and counted as the years passed. They knew Jeremiah's prophecy and believed that God would fulfill his promise to return them to the land (Jer. 25:11, 12; 29:10).

The following questions will be addressed in this section of the study: What was the experience of the Jews following their return from Babylon? In what ways, if any, did they experience the fulfillment of prophecy, and what challenges did they face?

## Events Leading up to the Rebuilding of the Temple

An initial event that in time led to the rebuilding of the temple was the Decree of Cyrus:

The Lord, the God of heaven, has given me all the kingdoms of the earth and he has appointed me to build a temple for him at Jerusalem in Judah. Anyone of his people among you—may his God be with him, and let him go up to Jerusalem in Judah and build the temple of the Lord, the God of Israel, the God who is in Jerusalem. And the people of any place where survivors may now be living are to provide him with silver and gold, with goods and livestock, and with freewill offerings for the temple of God in Jerusalem (Ezra 1:2-4).

With the arrival of King Cyrus, the world changed dramatically. Babylon was overthrown, along with its god, Marduk. Earlier policies were reversed. People were sent back to their homeland. A new world order was established. From a biblical perspective, God used the pagan king, Nebuchadnezzar, to judge and scatter his people (Jer 25:9; 27:6). Now, however, he worked through another king, Cyrus, to return his people to their land. Cyrus opened the door not only for the Jewish exiles to return to the land, but under his authority to rebuild the temple. He also provided for its construction and adornment.[225]

As noted in our texts, the return was interpreted by the returning remnant as divinely orchestrated. God worked through people and events, in particular through King Cyrus. From a human standpoint, several factors may have contributed to Cyrus's interest in seeing the temple in Jerusalem rebuilt. First, according to the famous Cylinder of Cyrus, found in Babylon in 1879, Cyrus refers to the fact that "he restored cults and returned exiled peoples to their homes."[226] In contrast to the earlier Assyrian rulers who conquered and scattered, Cyrus worked to restore order, portraying himself as a particularly benevolent ruler.

---

[225] James Trotter argues, unconvincingly, that "the impetus for the construction of the temple in Jerusalem came entirely from the [Persian] imperial center rather than from the Yehudites themselves." James M. Trotter, "Was the Second Jerusalem Temple a Primarily Persian Project?" *SJOT* 15 (2001): 287-294.

[226] Amélie Kuhrt, "The Cyrus Cylinder and Achaemenid Imperial Policy," *JSOT* 25 (1983): 84.

Second, certain scholars have argued that the ancient Persian rulers maintained a kindly attitude toward others who practiced monotheism. Amélie Kuhrt, for example, says that "the specific interest shown by Cyrus in the Jerusalem cult could be attributable to the fact that, as the Persians practiced an ethical monotheism, the Old Persian rulers would recognize the Jerusalem cult as one more in line with their own religion."[227]

Third, some have suggested that this action by Cyrus was part of the Old Persian policy to "establish support near a frontier in a politically sensitive zone (if one thinks of its proximity to Egypt) and bordering an area inhabited by the Arab tribes, a population group that had already presented problems of political control to imperial structures."[228] Cyrus may have been particularly interested in strengthening his western border.

Fourth, in another article that discusses the Cyrus Cylinder, Lisbeth Fried suggests that the temple in Jerusalem was built to increase "income to the crown."[229] In this same article Fried states,

> If the empire wanted to populate a locality, a temple to the local god had to be built. People would not move into an area without a home for their god. This may be why the Persians built and supported the Jerusalem temple: they wanted Judah populated . . . . The creation of a population center leads to the development of agriculture and markets and to an overall increase in wealth and income for the crown.[230]

---

[227] Ibid.

[228] Ibid., 94.

[229] Lisbeth S. Fried, "The House of the God Who Dwells in Jerusalem," *JAOS* 126, no. 1 (2006): 96.

[230] Ibid., 98.

Another author, John Betlyon, adds support to Fried's argument:

Judah, now called Yehud, indicating the influence of Persia's lingua franca, Aramaic, was a region particularly well suited to viticulture and cultivation of the olive. These crops had long been grown successfully for trade as well as local use. They would eventually enable Yehud to grow in economic importance and strength in its role as a province (or subprovince, depending on whose nomenclature one uses) within the huge Persian satrapy, Abar-nahara, also an Aramaic name.[231]

Simple economics may explain Cyrus's motivation in wanting the temple in Jerusalem rebuilt.

Further, it is known that the Jews were not the only group taken captive to Babylon that eventually returned to their homeland. A Syrian community had a similar experience. Laurie Pearce describes still another exile group that returned from Babylon: "A notable example of such a community is that of the Mesopotamian town of Neirab, a town named for its population's original home in Syria. The Neirabeans appear to have returned to their homeland shortly after (and in much the same manner as) Judean deportees and their descendants returned to Judah."[232]

---

[231] John W. Betlyon, "A People Transformed: Palestine in the Persian Period," *NEA* 68 (2005): 6.

[232] Laurie E. Pearce, "New Evidence for Judeans in Babylonia," in *Judah and the Judeans in the Persian Period,* eds. Oded Lipschits and Manfred Oeming (Winona Lake: Eisenbrauns, 2006), 408.

# Prophetic Fulfillment

While all of the above factors can rightly be considered as elements weighing on the Persian decision to rebuild the Jerusalem temple, to the believing Jew it was Yahweh who moved the heart of Cyrus to see that the temple was rebuilt (see Isa. 45:1-7). A second event interpreted as a fulfillment of prophecy was the return led by Sheshbazzar. Here, God intervened in such a way that a select group of Jews returned to Jerusalem. The text says, "Then the family heads of Judah and Benjamin, and the priests and Levites—everyone whose heart God had moved—prepared to go up and build the house of the Lord in Jerusalem" (Ezra 1:5).

Therefore, the Decree of Cyrus and the return under Sheshbazzar can rightly be viewed as prophetically significant. Nonetheless, life in the land turned out to be extremely difficult. Every element of progress was fraught with difficulty. First, the *golah* encountered strong opposition to their plans of rebuilding the temple. The opposition came from the local population, in particular from the people of Samaria. This opposition was so severe that construction was halted for years, until the reign of Darius. At that point, God intervened and spoke to his people through the prophets Haggai and Zechariah; and work resumed. Finally, the temple project was completed. The completion of the temple can be viewed as the third prophetically significant event (Ezek. 36:10, 33).

Another prophetically significant event was the return of God's favor/blessing to the *golah* and to the land (Hag. 2:19). The significance of this event could not be overstated. Michael Brown says,

As a preliminary statement, it must be stressed that nothing was more important than securing the blessing of God in one's life or nation. All religious or superstitious peoples (in other words, virtually the entire ancient world, along with most of the world to this day) have actively sought the blessing of a specific deity or spirit, believing that this blessing will make them fertile, or prosper them, protect them, deliver them, heal them, preserve them, empower them, exalt them, favor them, or, possibly, bring about all the above. The blessing is thought of as tangible, its effects perceivable and, at times, measurable. The more powerful the deity, the more important the blessing.[233]

Further help in understanding the bibilical mindset in relation to blessing comes from Mary Anne Isaak, who writes in the journal *Direction,* "The patriarchal narrative clearly illustrates that there is never a one-to-one relationship between human and divine involvement in blessing. Blessing begins with God and is carried on by God. Human participation and response is crucial, yes, but it is not the hinge on which God offers and sustains blessing."[234]

For a generation the land had rested (2 Chron. 36:21), during which a remnant of Jews lived in Babylon, far from their home. Suddenly all that changed. God's promise of blessing surely brought new hope to the *golah*. The covenant curses were reversed, and blessing returned to the people and to the land.

---

[233]  Michael L. Brown, "ברך," *NIDOTTE*, 1:758.

[234]  Mary Anne Isaak, "Literary Structure and Theology of the Patriarchal Narratives: The Three-fold Blessing," *Dir* 24, no. 2 (1995): 73.

# Events Associated with the Rebuilding of the Wall

In writing on the significance of reconstructing the temple, John Betlyon states, "With the rebuilding of the Temple, the religious lives of the Jews once again focused on Jerusalem and cultic sacrifices."[235] The worship of Yahweh returned to its historic cultic site. However, more was needed for Jerusalem to truly become the recognized spiritual center, both for Jews living in and around Yehud and for the larger diaspora community. Betlyon continues, "Early-fifth-century Jerusalem, however, was but a shadow of its late-seventh-century self."[236]

Years of frustration and distress followed. The *golah* needed both spiritual and physical help, but where would it come from? One can picture the people crying out to God. God's answer came through two specially prepared leaders, Ezra and Nehemiah, who brought spiritual and physical restoration to the city. Both of these men were closely associated with the Persian administration and served as loyal subjects to its rulers. Betlyon comments,

> Ezra, priest and scribe of the God of heaven, was sent to Jerusalem on an official mission to reform local religious and legal praxis. Ezra was followed in the mid-440s by Nehemiah, another official of the Persian crown. Nehemiah was given the dual charge of rebuilding the walls of Jerusalem and increasing the city's population.[237]

---

[235] Betlyon, "A People Transformed," 7.

[236] Ibid.

[237] Ibid.

With the arrival of these two leaders, would prophecy finally be fulfilled? Would Zion become the place where Yahweh's glorious presence resided once again? Would the glories of the Davidic kingdom return to the nation? These and other similar questions must have been part of the community's reflection. The group that returned with Ezra traveled with anticipation and hope. As Psalm 126:1-3 says,

> When the Lord brought back the captives to Zion, we were like men who dreamed. Our mouths were filled with laughter, our tongues with songs of joy. Then it was said among the nations, 'The Lord has done great things for them.' The Lord has done great things for us, and we are filled with joy.

These words reflect the sentiment of the Jews who returned from captivity. Unfortunately, it appears that their joy was short-lived. Problems arose. Both Ezra and Nehemiah were forced to confront not only the external problems threatening the community, but also the thorny internal issues within the *golah* community. The writings of the Second Temple era reflect the struggle felt within the Jewish community as it sought to understand its place in history. Roy Ciampa describes the theology behind penitential prayers:

> The penitential prayer tradition, reflected in Ezra 9, Nehemiah 1, 9, Daniel 9, and in several Jewish texts of the Second Temple period, suggests the same sense that the time of exile is coming (or should be coming) to an end, and yet that it is not quite over, or at least that the covenant curses have not yet ceased, and that the sins

of the people have not yet been fully forgiven (thus the penitential prayers confessing those sins and seeking that forgiveness). The prayers themselves reflect a theology based on an understanding of the proper response to the curse of exile . . . . The penitential prayer tradition is related to the motif of repentance as a prerequisite for restoration after the people failed to repent when warned by the prophets of the exile. Israel continues to confess its sins, since 'the ultimate *ma'al* [sin against God] which led to the exile . . . demanded a penitential confession to restore covenantal relationship.'[238]

The *golah* experienced disappointment. How were they to reconcile the difference between the life that they anticipated and the reality with which they lived? Conditions were difficult. Life was hard. Humility and repentance were needed. However, as promised, they had returned. Their time in Babylon had produced positive changes in their social and spiritual lives. In fact, they experienced partial fulfillment of the prophetic promises that included such things as the return, the removal of idols, the rebuilding of the temple, and the return of blessing. However, not all the promises of Jeremiah 30 and 31 and Ezekiel 37 were fulfilled. Much still remained unfinished. There must have been a sense of the "already but not yet."

Two major issues arose during this era that threatened the well-being and even existence of the *golah* community of Yehud. Both of these issues had to be addressed if Jerusalem was to serve

---

[238] Roy E. Ciampa, "The History of Redemption," in *Central Themes in Biblical Theology,* ed. Scott J. Hafemann and Paul R. House (Nottingham, England: Apollos, 2007), 286-287.

as the spiritual center of Judaism during the Persian era. The first issue was the problem of mixed marriages (Ezra 9:1). Philip Brown analyzes the significance of these mixed marriages:

The Israelites had intermarried with people who were practicing the same abominations that characterized the ancient Canaanites, Moabites, Ammonites, and Egyptians. Expanding the statement, one might read, 'The people of Israel and the priests and the Levites have not separated themselves from the peoples of the lands who act according to the abominations of the Canaanites, Hittites, Perizites, and Jebusites.'[239]

Describing the practices of these people, Brown adds, "Although sexual perversions are among the abominations of these people (Lev. 18:3-23), idolatry and its accompanying depravity are the primary items identified as their abominations."[240]

Both Ezra and Nehemiah recognized the threat that intermarriage with pagan women posed to the *golah*. In discussing the foreign women Brown writes, "When Nehemiah chastised the Jews who had married foreign women, he reminded them that Solomon's foreign wives turned his heart away from the Lord and caused him to sin despite the great favor he received from God."[241]

In relation to Ezra's concern about this issue Brown notes, "It was not intermarriage with foreigners as such that caused Ezra such consternation, but with foreigners who, whether

---

[239] Brown, "Mixed Marriages," 447-448.
[240] Ibid., 448.
[241] Ibid., 449.

syncretistic or pagan, were idolaters."[242] Brown interacts with Ezra's prayer saying, "From Ezra's vantage point the problem [of mixed marriage] was entirely spiritual in nature. The terms he used to describe it underscore the essentially spiritual nature of the problem: intermarriage with idolatrous women constituted unfaithfulness to Yahweh and abandonment of His commandments."[243]

Turning now to Ezra's time in Jerusalem, it is significant that Ezra arrived in Jerusalem with both spiritual passion and the full support of King Artaxerxes. According to the king's decree recorded in Ezra 7, Ezra was entrusted with the following authority: "Whoever does not obey the law of your God and the law of the king must surely be punished by death, banishment, confiscation of property, or imprisonment" (v.26). Consequently, Ezra was in a strong position to intervene against those who ignored or rejected God's laws. Therefore, Ezra did not hesitate to get involved directly with those Jews who had taken foreign wives.

The second religious issue related to the building of the wall was that of Sabbath. For Nehemiah, Sabbath-keeping was at the heart of Israel's covenantal identity. Sabbath-breaking was in essence apostasy (see Neh. 13:17-18). A major function for the wall was to control commerce and trade and keep foreigners, such as the men of Tyre, from selling their goods on the Sabbath. As Allen and Laniak write in their commentary,

The nub of the problem was a Sabbath market in Jerusalem, though grape treading was also involved. They

---

[242] Ibid.

[243] Ibid., 450.

were breaking the traditional injunction against work on the Sabbath, including selling (see Amos 8:5) and the associated conveyance of goods for sale (see Jer. 17:21, 27). Nehemiah blamed the Judean nobles, who doubtless resided in Jerusalem and formed a council of elders, for not exercising their authority. His speech has Jeremiah 17:19-23, 27 in view, which closes with a threat to destroy the capital. With hindsight, the governor thought of what had happened in the year 587 and the disastrous aftermath that dogged Judah thereafter. Like Ezra in Ezra 9:14 (also compare 10:14), he warned of a fresh outbreak of divine wrath. Again he took matters into his own hands. He closed the city gates near the market on Friday evening when the Sabbath began and took the extra precaution of temporarily manning them with his own staff. He warned traders who lingered hopefully outside, scaring them off. Then he put Levites in charge of the gates on the Sabbath, regarding maintenance of its holiness as an extension of their religious duties.[244]

The Sabbath was designed to be a day set aside each week for worship, rest, and blessing for the people and their livestock. Nehemiah recognized the importance of the observance of this day for the spiritual and physical well-being of the entire community. He intervened to see it reestablished in Jerusalem.

---

[244]  Allen and Laniak, *Ezra,* 163.

# The Archaeological Record

This study turns next to the archaeological record looking for evidence that the *golah* experienced a spiritual transformation in Babylon and, in particular, that they abandoned all forms of idol worship. Prior to the Babylonian captivity, Judah had become thoroughly pagan. The people were attached to their idols, and their religious practices were similar, if not identical, to the rites of their pagan neighbors (Jer. 2:11; 16:18; 32:34; Ezek. 5:9; 6:9; 14: 5-6; 16:21).

Ephraim Stern describes preexilic conditions in Palestine in the century prior to Judah's final destruction. According to Stern, Judah and each of the seven surrounding nations "had its own independent cult, consisting of the worship of a pair of deities."[245]

He describes how each of these nations had its own distinct male deity, including YHWH for the Judeans and Samaritans. Interestingly, the chief female deity in all of these nations, including Judah, was Asherah.

Stern's research suggests that by the end of the seventh century B.C., worship among these eight nations had become remarkably similar. To the untrained eye, the religious activities of these nations would have appeared virtually indistinguishable. Stern adds, "In fact, the pagan cult unique to Judah is represented by a rich assemblage of clay figurines dating from the late eighth century down to the beginning of the sixth century B.C.E. These

---

[245] The eight nations included Judah, the Arameans, the Phoenicians, the Samaritans, the late Philistines, the Ammonites, the Moabites, and the Edomites. Stern, "Religious Revolution," 199.

figurines are distributed all over Judah . . . In short, they occur in all parts of Judah."[246] Idolatry in preexilic Judah was rampant.

From an archaeological standpoint, little is known concerning the religious practices in Palestine between the years 586 B.C. and 539 B.C. Stern describes this period as a vacuum.[247] However, following the Babylonian Captivity the archaeological landscape suddenly changes. Stern notes that as the Persian era begins, new types of clay figurines appear. These figurines no longer exhibit individual national characteristics but are produced in two styles,

> (a) the Phoenician style that preserves eastern elements, and (b) the western Greek style that becomes increasingly dominant throughout pagan Palestine (in the areas outside of Judah and Samaria) and lacks nearly all regional or local characteristics . . . .

> In the areas of the country inhabited by Jews during the Persian Period, on the other hand, not a single cultic figurine or sanctuary has been found! This, in spite of the many excavations and surveys that have been conducted, and the same is true of Samaria.[248]

While no cultic figurines have been found in the areas inhabited by Jews during the Persian Period, the archeological record points

---

[246]  Ibid., 200.

[247]  Stern also notes that the Babylonians not only destroyed Judah but also exiled the Philistines, who never returned. Additionally, he notes that the Edomites occupied the southern part of Judah.

[248]  Ibid., 201.

to Jewish worship concentrated in two temples, the temple in Jerusalem and Samaritan temple found on Mt Gerizim.

The archaeological record demonstrates that other changes occurred in Judea and Samaria in the early Persian Period. One important development of that period was the introduction of coinage. Writing on this topic John Betlyon states,

> Coins were first introduced in the seventh century BCE in Asia Minor. Their initial use was probably to facilitate the payment of taxes to local governing authorities . . . .
>
> As Persian hegemony moved westward, Persian authorities came into closer contact with coined money. They realized the advantage of coinage not only for the payment of taxes due their government, but also to facilitate the exchange of goods and services. The old barter economy was slowly replaced by a fledgling monetary economy. This transformation would take centuries, particularly in inland areas far from prominent trade routes and access to the sea and international trade. But this change in how the world did "business" began in the sixth and fifth centuries BCE.[249]

Three differing weight standards were used in the coinage of the eastern Mediterranean region: the Athenian standard, the Persian standard, and the Phoenician standard. Large mints and also local smaller mints struck coins. As Betlyon says, "Coins struck in local Palestinian mints, including Gaza, Ashkelon,

---

[249] Betlyon, "A People Transformed," 47.

Jerusalem, and Samaria, were struck on either the Phoenician or Athenian standards."[250]

The coins struck in Jerusalem and Samaria appear to have been minted under the auspices of their respective temple authorities. According to Stern,

> The centrality of the Temple of Jerusalem and its function are attested, among other things, by several Yehud coins bearing names of priests, such as the well-known coin of Yohanan the priest and that of Jadoa, and others. These coins attest that at least some of them were struck by the priesthood for the benefit of the Temple, and it can be assumed that Jerusalem and its Temple fulfilled a decisive role not only in the religious life of the country but also in its economy.[251]

Recent excavations of the Samaritan Temple on Mount Gerizim have found that "among the large number of Samaritan coins discovered there were some Judean coins (which may indicate the existence of contacts between them and, perhaps, also visits by Jewish pilgrims to Mount Gerizim)."[252] The discovery of these coins may point to periods of rapprochement between Jerusalem and Samaria.[253] Betlyon suggests that the Jews of Yehud may

---

[250]  Ibid., 48.

[251]  Stern, "Persian-Period Judah," 202.

[252]  Ibid.

[253]  An additional factor of historical significance is that the people living in Samaria in the early Persian Period were culturally different from the later Samaritans of the first century AD.

have sought to "win over the Jews of Samaria to worship in the Jerusalem temple."[254]

What is certain is that the religious belief system of Samaria went through a major transformation from polytheism to monotheism during the Persian era. Describing this transformation Stern writes, "More than 300 monumental stone-carved inscriptions of different periods [have been uncovered]."[255] In addition, three important limestone capitals have been found. About these discoveries Stern states, "In my opinion, these capitals attest to an early pagan phase of the Temple on Mount Gerizim, before it became a center of monotheistic religion in the Persian Period."[256]

These discoveries are important, for they suggest that a robust spiritual life existed in Judea during the early Persian era that impacted their neighbors in Samaria. Jerusalem's commitment to monotheism spread to its neighbors.

Finally, Stern highlights an additional discovery with important implications relative to the spiritual health of the Persian era Jews in Jerusalem. He begins by noting that "the Jewish community in the Persian Period was dispersed in three areas. In addition to the Jewish center in Jerusalem and Yehud, Jews also lived in the Babylonian diaspora (where the new Jewish religion was developed) and in the Egyptian diaspora."[257] That there was communication between Jerusalem Jews and those living in Egypt is affirmed by documents such as the Passover Letter. Additionally, seal impressions from Yehud have been

---

254  Betlyon, "A People Transformed," 27.

255  Stern, "Persian-Period Judah," 202.

256  Ibid.

257  Ibid., 203.

discovered in excavations both in Babylon and in Kadesh-Barnea, which is on the route commonly taken to Egypt. Stern says,

> There is no doubt that these impressions were imprinted on wine jars, but, in my opinion, it seems completely irrational to transport by land over great distances this type of fragile pottery filled with wine only for the purpose of paying taxes (when we also know that the Persians demanded and received taxes from remote areas only in silver and gold). I therefore wish to propose here that it was the Jews in the Egyptian and Babylonian diaspora who imported the wine from Judah for religious purposes, wine that was in no danger of having been touched by heathen hands.[258]

It seems likely that wine along with bread was used in special religious ceremonies commemorating events such as Abraham's fellowship with Melchizedek and the Exodus. For diaspora Jews, wine bottled under the auspices of the Jerusalem Temple must have been esteemed as holding significant spiritual value.

In summary, this chapter has demonstrated how God used people and historical events, such as Cyrus and his decree, to fulfill the prophecy that a group of Jews would return to the land of promise and rebuild the temple. Jerusalem was reestablished as the spiritual center of Judaism. The rebuilding of the wall around the city provided security and allowed for the observation of religious rites and privileges in accordance with Torah.

The archaeological record suggests that a spiritually strong and active religious community lived in Jerusalem during this era.

---

[258]   Ibid.

Evidence for this claim includes Samaria's return to monotheism and the removal of all forms of idol worship in both Judea and Samaria. Further, the *golah's* commitment to God and their fellow Jews is evidenced by their provision of consecrated wine for the spiritual health of the Jewish communities living in Babylon and Egypt.

# Chapter 6

# Conclusions

This study began with the idea that Israel's time in Babylon followed by the return, though fraught with challenges, holds immense prophetic value and needs to be understood as part of God's larger redemptive program, first for Israel and ultimately for the nations. This has not been the consensus view over the past two centuries, especially among those who have employed the analysis of the German scholar Julius Wellhausen.

In his investigation of this period, Wellhausen began by noting the adverse circumstances into which the *golah* returned following their time in Babylon. As he described it, life for the returnees was drab, without security or joy. He followed his description of the return with a compelling rhetorical question: "Were these then the Messianic times which, it had been foretold, were to dawn at the close of their captivity?"[259]

At this point Wellhausen appears to have the rhetorical and theological high ground from which he can paint his picture of

---

[259] Wellhausen, *Prolegomena*, 494.

the Second Temple era. Here, then, is Wellhausen's depiction of early Second Temple Judaism.

First, to one side sits the Jewish remnant community. They are depicted hovering off in a dark corner with heads down, hopeless and despairing. They are unforgiven. Using Wellhausen's words, "The sins of God's people seemed still unforgiven, their period of bond-service not yet at an end."[260]

Second, there is God who sits far off in the distance with his back to everyone and everything. He is sullen and aloof. According to Wellhausen, despite every effort of the Jewish remnant community to assuage their deity, he "refused to be mollified."[261] Third, in the center of the picture above everything else sits a large and gaudy crown with an unmistakable P written on it, the Persian monarchy. Wellhausen stated, "The Persian yoke pressed now more heavily than ever the Babylonian had done [upon its subjects]."[262]

Fourth, in the center and below the crown sits a rather small, yet pretentious-looking Jewish man. He occupies a throne on which he sits waiting for his scurrying little Levite servants to carry out his every wish. He is pompous, unsmiling, and dressed in the attire of a medieval pope. In his right hand, he holds a scroll with the Hebrew letter "ד," for *D'varim* (Deuteronomy), written on it. Under his left hand sits a man dressed in the garments of a prophet with a tiny "e" on his front that can be seen only with intense effort: Ezekiel. To quote Wellhausen, "The hierocracy towards which Ezekiel had already opened the way was simply inevitable. It took the form of a monarchy of the high priest, he

---

260  Ibid.
261  Ibid., 495.
262  Ibid., 494.

having stepped into the place formerly occupied by the theocratic king."[263]

This is Wellhausen's portrayal of the early Second Temple era. It has survived for well over a century with amazing resilience. But is it correct? While the return from Babylon did not usher in the Messianic age, neither did the *golah* live in a constant state of hopeless isolation, unforgiveness and despair. Further, Wellhausen's analysis and conclusions are unsustainable for the following reasons.

First, in Babylon the Jews gained a new understanding of Yahweh as not simply the national God of Israel, but rather as the God who rules over history and controls the destiny of individuals, families, peoples and nations. Nehemiah, in his prayer, referred to God as the "God of heaven, the great and awesome God, who keeps his covenant of love with those who love him and obey his commands" (Neh. 1:5). The *golah* saw Milcom of the Ammonites, Chemosh of the Moabites, Qos of the Edomites, and Ba'al of the Phoenicians as utterly useless idols when compared to YHWH, the living God of Israel.

The exiles in Babylon learned that God is to be revered and feared, for not only is he a God of "covenant love," *hsd*, but he is also a God who follows through with his promise to judge his rebellious people with covenantal curses. For example, he did not hesitate to use an ungodly king like Nebuchadnezzar, calling him *'bdi*, "my servant," to severely discipline his people.

This new understanding of God gave rise to a new knowledge of genuine repentance. For Israel, this repentance led to restoration. Both Jeremiah and Ezekiel called for and explained this way of repentance. The classic example came through the prophetic

---

[263]  Ibid., 495.

words of Ephraim: "After I strayed, I repented; after I came to understand, I beat my breast. I was ashamed and humiliated because I bore the disgrace of my youth" (Jer. 31:19). Through Ezekiel God said, "'For I take no pleasure in the death of anyone,' declares the Sovereign LORD. 'Repent and live!'" (Ezek. 18:32). That the exiles finally grasped this idea is reflected in God's word through the prophet Zechariah: "But did not my words and my decrees, which I commanded my servants the prophets, overtake your forefathers? Then they repented and said, 'The LORD Almighty has done to us what our ways and practices deserve, just as he determined to do'" (Zech. 1:6).

This theology of repentance is reflected in the prayer of Ezra:

O my God, I am too ashamed and disgraced to lift up my face to you, my God, because our sins are higher than our heads and our guilt has reached to the heavens. From the days of our forefathers until now, our guilt has been great. Because of our sins, we and our kings and our priests have been subjected to the sword and captivity, to pillage and humiliation at the hand of foreign kings, as it is today.

But now, for a brief moment, the Lord our God has been gracious in leaving us a remnant and giving us a firm place in his sanctuary, and so our God gives light to our eyes and a little relief in our bondage. Though we are slaves, our God has not deserted us in our bondage. He has shown us kindness in the sight of the kings of Persia. He has granted us new life to rebuild the house of our God and repair its ruins, and he has given us a wall of protection in Judah and Jerusalem (Ezra 9:6-9).

This was a theology of hope based on repentance and on the goodness and kindness of God. This was part of postexilic theology.

Next, as Wellhausen correctly recognized, the postexilic social and political structure was very different from that of the preexilic period. There was, in fact, a new world order. The Davidic monarchy with its line of kings no longer reigned. In the postexilic era there was no kingdom, only a remnant living back in the land under the authority of a series of Persian-appointed governors. These governors, however, had an interest in the well-being of the local population. As Ernest-Marie Laperrousaz has demonstrated, "Ainsi, jusqu'à la fin de l'époque perse se trouve attestée l'existence de gouveneurs juifs de la province de Judée." (Thus, until the end of the Persian era [the record] attests to the existence of Jewish governors in the province of Judea.)[264] These Jewish governors, including Zerubbabel and Nehemiah, were sensitive to the interests of the Jewish community in Yehud. Consequently, to conclude, as Wellhausen does, that the Jewish high priest maintained monarchical authority during the Persian era is flawed.[265] Some form of power-sharing certainly existed

---

[264] Ernest-Marie Laperrousaz, "Le Régime Théocratique Juif a-t-il Commencé a l'Époque Perse, ou Seulemant a l'Époque Hellénistique?" (Did the Jewish Theocratic Governance begin in the Persian era or only in the Hellenistic era?) *Sem* 32 (1982): 95. For further discussion on the Jewish governors of Judah during the Persian era along with an analysis of Albrecht Alt's argument that the leaders who preceded Nehemiah were not truly governors but were only "special commissioners," see Hugh G.M. Williamson, "The Governors of Judah Under the Persians," *TynBul* 39 (1988): 59-82.

[265] The later governmental power structure that existed under the Greeks and Romans deserves further investigation.

between the high priest and the Persian-appointed governor. The high priest did not have absolute authority.

Turning to the remnant, it is important to recognize that this group was indeed significant in God's larger plan for Israel. They had gone through the Babylonian exile and survived. This was the group designated by God as the "good figs" of Jeremiah 24 that would "return to [him] with all their heart." In Babylon they witnessed, firsthand, God's judgment on the false prophets and the leaders guilty of leading God's people astray (see Jer. 29:20-32). Planted within the heart of this group was knowledge of God's sovereignty over human history. Yahweh, to them, was both Israel's God and the God who rules the nations. He fulfilled his promise to them both in regard to the exile and the return. They returned to the land knowing that they were to rid it of idols and also rebuild the temple (see Ezek. 11:18; Ezra 1:5).

Second, the Jews went into the Babylonian captivity in a proud and rebellious state. By contrast, they returned to the land in humility and in awe of Yahweh (Ps. 126:1-3). In Babylon they rejected the preexilic belief system, with its three major tenets—that idols were efficacious, that both the temple building and the Davidic line of rulers would remain forever, and that Israel could rely on foreign alliances for survival. Through the events that led up to and included the exile, they recognized that their idols were worthless. To their shame, they had even sacrificed their children to idols (Ezek. 16:21). Furthermore, the temple was destroyed, the king was taken into exile, and their alliance with Pharaoh failed.

Third, within the exile community there developed a recognition, respect, and reverence for God's written word. Torah, Yahweh's living word of instruction, became a unifying force among the exiled Jews. This new appreciation for Torah gave rise to a new mindset and receptiveness to the commands and requirements of God. An example of the importance of Torah within the postexilic society is seen in the life of Ezra. Ezra is described as "a teacher well versed in the Law of Moses" (7:6) who "had devoted himself to the study and observance of the Law of the Lord, and to teaching its decrees and laws in Israel" (7:10). This recognition of the strategic place held by the written word is further illustrated in Neh. 8:5: "Ezra opened the book. All the people could see him because he was standing above them; and as he opened it, the people all stood up." God's written word was held in high esteem.

Fourth, a sense of prophetic fulfillment motivated Israel's return to the land. The Book of Ezra begins with the proclamation of Cyrus that opened the way for the Jews in Babylon to return to Jerusalem. Next, v. 5 of the same chapter says, "Then the family heads of Judah and Benjamin, and the priest and Levites—everyone whose heart God had moved—prepared to go up and build the house of the Lord in Jerusalem." Later, Ezra traveled to Jerusalem with a similar sense of prophetic fulfillment motivating his trip. After recording the letter written by Artaxerxes on his behalf, Ezra adds his evaluation:

> Praise be to the Lord, the God of our fathers, who has put it into the king's heart to bring honor to the house of the Lord in Jerusalem in this way and who has extended his good favor to me before the king and his advisors and all the king's powerful officials. Because the hand of the Lord my God was on me, I took courage and gathered leading men from Israel to go up with me (Ezra 7:27-28).

Fifth, as described in chapters 3 and 4, the postexilic texts carry a strong undercurrent of reversal. This began with the Decree of Cyrus that opened the way for the Jewish exiles to return home. In addition, Cyrus "brought out the articles belonging to the temple of the Lord, which Nebuchadnezzar had carried away from Jerusalem and placed them in the temple of his god" (Ezra 1:7). Other examples of reversal include the promise of blessing that began on the day when the foundation of the temple was laid (Hag. 2:18-19) and the promise made to Zerubbabel, reversing the curse placed on his descendant, King Jehoiachin (Hag. 2:23). This undercurrent of reversal is particularly noticeable in Zechariah 8 where God says,

> Just as I had determined to bring disaster upon you and showed no pity when your fathers angered me, says the Lord Almighty, so now I have determined to do good again to Jerusalem and Judah. Do not be afraid (vv.14-15).

Sixth, a strong commitment to individual and corporate prayer and worship developed in Babylon. The importance of individual prayer is reflected in the request of Nehemiah (chapter 1), where he petitions God for favor with the Persian king so that he would be allowed to go and rebuild the wall around Jerusalem. The importance of corporate prayer can be seen in Nehemiah 9, where after recounting God's faithfulness and Israel's rebellion, the text in v. 38 says, "In view of all this, we are making a binding agreement, putting it in writing, and our leaders, our Levites and our priests are affixing their seals to it." Corporate prayer led to the writing of a covenant of commitment between the people and God.

Also, united corporate worship served to bond the *golah* with the extended Jewish community that lived in and around Jerusalem. After recording the size of the original *golah* community—42,360 (Neh. 7:66), the text reports in 8:1, "When the seventh month came and the Israelites had settled in their towns, all the people assembled as one man in the square before the Water Gate."[266] Nehemiah's text points to the fact that almost 100 years after the initial return from Babylon, the *golah* community continued to exhibit spiritual health and unity. This was displayed in their corporate worship.

After Ezra recounts the completion and dedication of the temple, he describes the Passover celebration that followed (Ezra 6). He writes, "So the Israelites who had returned from the exile ate [the Passover meal], together with all who had separated themselves from the unclean practices of their Gentile neighbors in order to seek the Lord, the God of Israel" (Ezra 6:21). This text points to worship and renewal occurring simultaneously.

Seventh, the extended postexilic Jewish community lived with the promise of joy and blessing. For example, God promised that the fasts, which had previously been times of mourning and sadness, would be transformed into times of joy and celebration. In Zechariah 8:19 the text says, "This is what the Lord Almighty says: 'The fasts of the fourth, fifth, seventh and tenth months will become joyful and glad occasions and happy festivals for Judah. Therefore love truth and peace.'" Joy replaced sadness and mourning.

---

[266] It should be noted that most Hebrew manuscripts do not include this last verse. However, even if this verse is not accepted as part of the original text, the verses that follow underscore both the size of the assembly and the fact that the people listened and responded attentively to the reading of Torah.

Another important promise given to this group was the promise of blessing in Haggai 2:18-19: "From this day on, from this twenty-fourth day of the ninth month . . . From this day on I will bless you." Instead of "refusing to be mollified," God lavishly extended his favor and blessing to his people.

In summary, these seven areas point to the fact that genuine spiritual and societal transformation took place in Babylon, so much so that the postexilic Jewish community moved beyond the covenant curses to a time where the *golah* community experienced God's shalom and favor. Unfortunately, Wellhausen failed to recognize this transformation.

In addition to the reasons given above, Wellhausen's myopic approach to interpreting the exile and return cannot be sustained in that he overlooks the larger picture of God's redemptive activity being worked out in history. His all-or-nothing approach leaves no room for other options, such as that of partial fulfillment. As was presented at the end of the first chapter, the preexilic prophets Jeremiah and Ezekiel, present a large picture of history and the direction toward which history is moving. Their vision may be summarized by the following chiasm:

A. David shepherds all of Israel
   B. The kingdom separates into Israel and Judah
      C. Israel goes into captivity
         D. Judah is taken into captivity
            E. In Babylon, a spiritual transformation occurs
         D'. A remnant of Judah returns from captivity
      C'. Greater Israel returns from captivity
         (Jer. 30:3; 50:4-5)
   B'. The two kingdoms are formally reunited (Ezek. 37:15-22)
A'. Messianic David shepherds all of Israel (Ezek. 37:24-25)

Finally, the text of Scripture and the analysis of this study point to the necessity of two distinct returns to the land—one near and one distant. The near return was worked out historically following the Decree of Cyrus when Sheshbazzar led the first group out of Babylon and back to Jerusalem (Ezra 1:5-11). This return, while limited in scope and rather small in size, served to foreshadow a future and glorious return that still awaits fulfillment (Jer. 30:3; 31:8-11; Ezek. 36:24-28; Zech. 8:7-8). In a recent article, Walter Kaiser provides the following insight:

> The return from the 70 years of captivity in Babylon did not completely fulfill what God had promised. If it had, then why was the prophet Zechariah (Zech 10:8-12) still predicting this return to the land once again as late as 518 B.C., some 18 years after the return from Babylon? Well after the days when Judah had returned from Babylonian captivity, the prophet Zechariah was still repeating this same ancient promise of God.[267]

The idea of two returns did not originate with Kaiser, but has deep historic roots. Referring to Israel's promised return in Deuteronomy, David Lambert writes, "[T]he medieval exegete Naḥmanides, maintained that Deut. 4:29-31 refers to the historical return to Zion after the destruction of the First Temple, whereas Deut. 30:1-10 refers to the eschatological in-gathering of the exiles

------

[267] Walter C. Kaiser Jr., "Israel and Its Land in Biblical Perspective." in *The Old Testament in the Life of God's People: Essays in Honor of Elmer A. Martens,* ed. Jon Isaak (Winona Lake: Eisenbrauns, 2009), 256.

from the current Diaspora."[268] The idea of two returns has long been proposed as part of God's overall plan for Israel.

In conclusion, this study has sought to provide evidence showing that Israel's time in Babylon served both a redemptive and a prophetic purpose. Following the death of King Josiah, the kingdom of Judah moved rapidly toward social and spiritual disintegration. However, in Babylon God intervened through his Word, his Spirit, and the voice of his prophets to bring about a transformation. The transformation occurred when the exiled Jewish remnant repented and returned to their covenant with Yahweh. Consequently, a living relationship with Yahweh resulted that was passed on to succeeding generations throughout the Second Temple era.

An enormous amount of research and analysis remains for those who would continue this study, looking not only into the Persian period but also into the Greek and Roman eras to examine how this remnant survived within the context of ongoing change and the pressure to conform to different thought systems, social structures, and world views.

---

[268] David Lambert. "Did Israel Believe that Redemption Awaited Its Repentance? The Case of *Jubilees* 1." *CBQ* 68 (2006): 634.

# BIBLIOGRAPHY

## Books


Ackroyd, Peter R. *Israel under Babylon and Persia*. London: Oxford University Press, 1970.

__________. *The Chronicler in His Age*. Sheffield: Sheffield Academic Press, 1991.

Albertz, Rainer. *Israel in Exile: The History and Literature of the Sixth Century B.C.E.* Atlanta: Society of Biblical Literature, 2003.

Allen, Leslie C. and Timothy S. Laniak. *Ezra, Nehemiah, Esther*. New International Biblical Commentary. Peabody, MA: Hendrickson Publishers, 2003.

Baldwin, Joyce G. *Haggai, Zechariah, Malachi*. Tyndale Old Testament Commentary. Downers Grove: InterVarsity Press, 1972.

Becking, Bob and Marjo C. A. Korpel, eds. *The Crisis of Israelite Religion*. Leiden: Brill, 1999.

Berquist, Jon L. *Judism in Persia's Shadow: A Social and Historical Approach*. Minneapolis: Fortress Press, 1995.

Blenkinsopp, Joseph. *Ezekiel*. Louisville: John Knox Press, 1990.

__________. *Sage—Priest—Prophet: Religious and Intellectual Leadership in Ancient Israel*. Louisville: Westminster John Knox Press, 1995.

Block, Daniel I. *The Book of Ezekiel: Chapters 1-24*. Grand Rapids: Wm. B. Eerdmans, 1997.

__________. *The Book of Ezekiel: Chapters: 25-48*. Grand Rapids: Wm. B. Eerdmans, 1998.

Boda, Mark J. *Haggai & Zechariah Research: A Bibliographic Survey*. Leiden: Deo Publishing, 2003.

Bright, John. *A History of Israel*. Philadelphia: Westminster Press, 1981.

__________. *Covenant and Promise: The Prophetic Understanding of the Future in Preexilic Israel*. Philadelphia: Westminster Press, 1976.

Brueggemann, Walter. *A Commentary on Jeremiah: Exile and Homecoming*. Grand Rapids: Wm. B. Eerdmans, 1998.

__________. *An Introduction to the Old Testament*. Louisville: Westminster John Knox Press, 2003.

__________. *Old Testament Theology*. Minneapolis: Fortress Press, 1992.

Bryan, Steven M. *Jesus and Israel's Traditions of Judgement and Restoration*. Cambridge: Cambridge University Press, 2002.

Childs, Brevard S. *Introduction to the Old Testament as Scripture*. Philadelphia: Fortress Press, 1979.

Coogan, Michael D., ed. *The Oxford History of the Biblical World*. New York: Oxford University Press, 1998.

Cook, Stephen L. *Prophecy and Apocalypticism: The Postexilic Social Setting*. Minneapolis: Fortress Press, 1995.

Cooper, Lamar Eugene Sr. *Ezekiel*. The New American Commentary 17, edited by E. Ray Clendenen. Nashville: Broadman and Holman, 1994.

Craigie, Peter C. *Ezekiel*. Philadelphia: The Westminster Press, 1983.

Dumbrell, William J. *Covenant and Creation: An Old Testament Covenantal Theology.* Carlisle, England: The Paternoster Press, 1984.

__________. *The Faith of Israel: A Theological Survey of the Old Testament.* Grand Rapids: Baker Academic, 2002.

Eichrodt, Walther. *Ezekiel.* London: SCM Press, 1970

Elledge, C.D. *The Bible and the Dead Sea Scrolls.* Atlanta: Society of Biblical Literature, 2005.

Feinberg, Charles Lee. *The Prophecy of Ezekiel.* Chicago: Moody Press, 1969.

__________. *Jeremiah: A Commentary.* Grand Rapids: Zondervan, 1982.

Fishbane, Michael. *Biblical Interpretation in Ancient Israel.* Oxford: Clarendon Press, 1985.

Floyd, Michael H. *Minor Prophets: Part 2.* The Forms of the Old Testament Literature XXII, edited by Rolf P. Knierim, Gene M. Tucker, and Marvin A. Sweeney. Grand Rapids: Wm B. Eerdmans, 1999.

Grabbe, Lester L. *A History of the Jews and Judaism in the Second Temple Period.* Vol. 1. New York: T&T Clark, 2004.

Hafeman, Scott J. and Paul R. House eds. *Central Themes in Biblical Theology.* Nottingham, England: Apollos, 2007.

Hafeman, Scott J. *Paul, Moses, and the History of Israel.* Peabody, MA: Hendrickson Publishers, 1996.

Hals, Ronald M. *Ezekiel.* Grand Rapids: Wm. B. Eerdmans, 1988.

Harris, R. Laird, ed. *Theological Wordbook of the Old Testament.* Chicago: Moody Press, 1980.

Hasel, Gerhard F. *The Remnant: The History and Theology of the Remnant Idea from Genesis to Isaiah.* Berrien Springs, MI: Andrews University Press, 1972.

Hess, Richard S. *Israelite Religions: An Archaeological and Biblical Survey*. Grand Rapids: Baker Academic, 2007.

Holloway, Steven W. and Lowell K. Handy. *The Pitcher is Broken: Memorial Essays for Gösta W. Ahlström*. Sheffield: Sheffield Academic Press, 1995.

House, Paul R. *Old Testament Theology*. Downers Grove: InterVarsity Press, 1998.

Huey, F.B. Jr. *Jeremiah and Lamentations*. The New American Commentary 16, edited by E. Ray Clendenen. Nashville: Broadman and Holman, 1993.

Huffmon, H.B., F.A. Spina, and A.R.W. Green. *The Quest for the Kingdom of God: Studies in Honor of George E. Mendenhall*. Winona Lake: Eisenbrauns, 1983.

Isaak, Jon, ed. *The Old Testament in the Life of God's People: Essays in Honor of Elmer A. Martens*. Winona Lake: Eisenbrauns, 2009.

Japhet, Sara. *From the Rivers of Babylon to the Highlands of Judah*. Winona Lake: Eisenbrauns, 2006.

Josephus, Falvius. *Complete Works/Josephus*. Translated by William Whiston. Grand Rapids: Kregel, 1978.

Kaiser, Walter C. *A History of Israel*. Nashville: Broadman and Holman, 1998.

__________. *Mission in the Old Testament: Israel as a Light to the Nations*. Grand Rapids: Baker Books, 2000.

__________. *The Messiah in the Old Testament*. Grand Rapids: Zondervan, 1995.

Kaufmann, Yehezkel. *The Religion of Israel*. Translated by Moshe Greenberg. Chicago: University of Chicago Press, 1960.

Keck, Leander E., ed. *The New Interpreter's Bible*. Vol. 7. Nashville: Abingdon Press, 1996.

Klein, Ralph W. *Ezekiel: The Prophet and His Message.* Columbia, S.C.: University of South Carolina Press, 1988.

Knowles, Melody D. *Centrality Practiced.* Atlanta: Society of Biblical Literature, 2006.

Lipschits, Oded. *The Fall and Rise of Jerusalem.* Winona Lake: Eisenbrauns, 2005.

Lipschits, Oded and Manfred Oeming, eds. *Judah and the Judeans in the Persian Period.* Winona Lake: Eisenbrauns, 2006.

Luker, Lamonte M., ed. *Passion, Vitality, and Foment: The Dynamics of Second Temple Judaism.* Harrisburg, PA: Trinity Press International, 2001.

Lundbom, Jack R. *Jeremiah 21-36.* The Anchor Bible Series. New York: Doubleday, 2004.

Martens, Elmer A. *God's Design: A Focus on Old Testament Theology.* Grand Rapids: Baker Books, 1981.

Matthews, Victor H. *Old Testament Themes.* St. Louis: Chalice Press, 2000.

McKane, William F.B.A. *A Critical and Exegetical Commentary on Jeremiah.* 2 vols. Edinburgh: T&T Clark, 1986.

Merrill, Eugene H. *Everlasting Dominion: A Theology of the Old Testament.* Nashville: Broadman and Holman, 2006.

Meyers, Carol L. and Eric M. Meyers. *Haggai, Zechariah 1-8.* The Anchor Bible. New York: Doubleday, 1987.

Middlemas, Jill. *The Templeless Age.* Louisville: Westminster John Knox Press, 2007.

Moberly, R.W.L. *The Old Testament of the Old Testament.* Minneapolis: Fortress Press, 1992.

Neusner, Jacob. *Foundations of Judaism.* Philadelphia: Fortress Press, 1989.

Newman, Carey C., ed. *Jesus & the Restoration of Israel.* Downers Grove: InterVarsity Press, 1999.

Newsome, James D. Jr. *By the Waters of Babylon: An Introduction to the History and Theology of the Exile*. Atlanta: John Knox Press, 1979.

Oswalt, John N. *The Book of Isaiah: Chapters 1-39*. Grand Rapids: Wm. B. Eerdmans, 1986

Peterson, David L. *Haggai, Zechariah 1-8,* Old Testament Library. Philadelphia: Westminster Press, 1984.

__________. *Prophecy in Israel: Search for an Identity*. Philadelphia: Fortress Press, 1986.

Redditt, Paul L. *Haggai, Zechariah and Malachi*. The New Century Bible Commentary Series. Grand Rapids: Wm. B. Eerdmans, 1995.

Reumann, John, ed. *The Promise and Practice of Biblical Theology*. Minneapolis: Fortress Press, 1991.

Rose, Wolter H. *Zemah and Zerubbabel: Messianic Expectations in the Early Postexilic Period*. Sheffield: Sheffield Academic Press, 2000.

Sacchi, Paolo. *The History of the Second Temple Period*. Sheffield: Sheffield Academic Press, 2000.

Sailhamer, John H. *Introduction to Old Testament Theology: A Canonical Approach*. Grand Rapids: Zondervan, 1995.

Sanders, E.P. *Judaism: Practice and Belief 63 BCE-66 CE*. London: SCM Press, 1992.

Stern, Ephraim. *Archaeology of the Land of the Bible*. The Anchor Bible Reference Library 11. New York: Doubleday, 2001.

Stuhlmueller, Carroll. *Rebuilding with Hope: A Commentary of the Books of Haggai and Zechariah*. Grand Rapids: Wm. B. Eerdmans, 1988.

Taylor, Richard A. and E. Ray Clendenen. *Haggai, Malachi*. The New American Commentary 21A, edited by E. Ray Clendenen. Nashville: Broadman and Holman, 2004.

Tollington, Janet A. *Tradition and Innovation in Haggai and Zechariah.* Sheffield: Sheffield Academic Press, 1993.

VanderKam, James C. *Calendars in the Dead Sea Scrolls: Measuring Time.* London: Routledge, 1998.

VanGemeren, Willem A. Gen., ed. *New International Dictionary of Old Testament Theology and Exegesis,* 5 vols. Grand Rapids: Zondervan, 1997.

Verhoef, Pieter A. *The Books of Haggai and Malachi.* Grand Rapids: Wm. B. Eerdmans, 1987.

Von Rad, Gerhardt. *Old Testament Theology.* 2 vol. San Francisco: Harper & Row, 1965.

Waltke, Bruce K. *An Old Testament Theology.* Grand Rapids: Zondervan, 2007.

Wellhausen, Julius. *Prolegomena to the History of Ancient Israel.* Edited by Harry W. Gilmer. Atlanta: Scholars Press, 1994.

Werline, Rodney Alan. *Penitential Prayer in Second Temple Judaism: The Development of a Religious Institution.* Atlanta: Scholars Press, 1998.

Westermann, Claus. *Prophetic Oracles of Salvation in the Old Testament.* Louisville: Westminster John Knox Press, 1991.

Wood, Leon J. *The Prophets of Israel.* Grand Rapids: Baker Books, 1979.

Wright, N.T. *Christian Origins and the Question of God.* Minneapolis: Fortress Press, 1992.

__________. *The New Testament and the People of God.* Vol. 1. Minneapolis: Fortress Press, 1992.

Yamauchi, Edwin M. *Persia and the Bible.* Grand Rapids: Baker Books, 1990.

Zimmerli, Walther. *Ezekiel 1: A Commentary on the Book of the Prophet Ezekiel, Chapters 1-24.* Translated by Roland E. Clements. Philadelphia: Fortress Press, 1979.

Zuck, Roy B., ed. *A Biblical Theology of the Old Testament.* Chicago: Moody Press, 1991.

Zucker, David J. *Israel's Prophets: An Introduction for Christians and Jews.* New York: Paulist Press, 1994.


# Articles


Abma, Richtsje. "Travelling from Babylon to Zion: Location and its Function in Isaiah 49-55." *JSOT* 74 (1997): 3-28.

Ackroyd, Peter R. "The Place of the Old Testament in the Church's Teaching and Worship." *ExpTim* 74 (1963): 164-167.

__________. "Two Old Testament Historical Problems of the Early Persian Period." *JNES* 17, no.1 (1958): 13-27.

Adeyemi, Femi. "What is the New Covenant 'Law' in Jeremiah 31:33?" *BSac* 163 (2006): 312-321.

Aitken, K. T. "שמע." *NIDOTTE,* 4:175-181. Grand Rapids: Zondervan, 1997.

Alexander, Ralph H. "ידה." *TWOT,* 1:364-366. Chicago: Moody Press, 1980.

Allen, Roland B. "עמד." *TWOT,* 2:675. Chicago: Moody Press, 1980.

Assis, Elie. "Haggai: Structure and Meaning." *Bib* 87, no.4 (2006): 531-541.

Atkinson, K.M.T. "The Legitimacy of Cambyses and Darius as Kings of Egypt." *JAOS* 76, no.3 (1956): 167-177.

Averbeck, Richard E. "מקדש." *NIDOTTE,* 2:1078-1087. Grand Rapids: Zondervan, 1997.

Baer, D. A. and R. P. Gordon, "חסד." *NIDOTTE,* 2:211-218. Grand Rapids: Zondervan, 1997.

Baldwin, Joyce G. "Malachi 1:11 and the Worship of the Nations in the Old Testament." *TynBul* 23 (1972): 117-124.

Barr, James. "Story and History in Biblical Theology." *JR* 56 (1976): 1-17.

Batto, Bernard F. "The Covenant of Peace: A Neglected Ancient Near East Motif." *CBQ* 49, no.2 (2006): 187-190.

Beaulieu, Paul-Alain. "An Episode in the Fall of Babylon to the Persians." *JNES* 52, no.4 (1993): 241-261.

Becking, Bob. "Continuity and Community: the Belief System of the Book of Ezra." In *The Crisis of Israelite Religion,* edited by Bob Becking and Marjo C.A. Korpel, 256-275. Leiden: Brill, 1999.

Bedford, Peter R. "Diaspora: Homeland Relations in Ezra-Nehemiah." *VT* 52, no.2 (2002): 147-156.

Begg, Christopher T. "The Significance of Jehoiachin's Release: A New Proposal." *JSOT* 36 (1986): 49-56.

Betlyon, John W. "A People Transformed: Palestine in the Persian Period." *NEA* 68 (2005): 4-58.

Blenkinsopp, J. "Old Testament Theology and the Jewish-Christian Connection." *JSOT* 28 (1984): 3-15.

__________. "The Bible, Archaeology and Politics; or The Empty Land Revisited." *JSOT* 27, no.2 (2002): 169-187.

__________. "The Judean Priesthood during the Neo-Babylonian and Achaemenid Periods: A Hypothetical Reconstruction." *CBQ* 60 (1998): 25-42.

__________. "The Social Roles of Prophets in Early Achaemenid Judah." *JSOT* 93 (2001): 39-58.

Block, Daniel I. "The Prophet of the Spirit: The Use of *RWḤ* in the Book of Ezekiel." *JETS* 32, no.1 (1989): 27-49.

Bloomhardt, Paul F. "The Poems of Haggai." *HUCA* 5 no.1 (1928): 153-180.

Bockmuehl, Markus. "Natural Law in Second Temple Judaism." *VT* 45, no.1 (1995): 17-44.

Boda, Mark J. "Haggai: Master Rhetorician." *TynBul* 51, no.2 (2000): 295-304.

__________. "Majoring on the Minors: Recent Research on Haggai and Zechariah." *CurBR* 2 (October 2003): 33-68.

__________. "Praying the Tradition: The Origin and Use of Tradition in Nehemiah 9." *TynBul* 48, no.1 (1997): 79-82.

__________. "Terrifying the Horns: Persia and Babylon in Zechariah 1:7-6:15." *CBQ* 67, no.1 (2005): 22-41.

Bowling, Andrew. "ירא." *TWOT,* 1:399-401. Chicago: Moody Press, 1980.

Brensinger Terry L. "חיה." *NIDOTTE,* 2:108-113. Grand Rapids: Zondervan, 1997.

Brettler, Marc Zvi. "Judaism in the Hebrew Bible? The Transition from Ancient Israelite Religion to Judaism." *CBQ* 61 (1999): 429-447.

Bright, John. "Faith and Destiny." *Int* 5, no.1 (1951): 3-26.

Brown, A. Philip II. "Nehemiah and Narrative Order in the Book of Ezra." *BSac* 162 (2005): 175-94.

__________. "The Problem of Mixed Marriages in Ezra 9-10." *BSac* 162 (2005): 437-58.

Brueggemann, Walter. "A Brief Moment for a One-Person Remnant (2 Kings 5:2-3)." *BTB* 31, no.2 (2001): 53-59.

__________. "(I)chabod Departed." *PSB* 22, no.1 (2001): 115-133.

Bruehler, Bart B. "Seeing through the עינים of Zechariah: Understanding Zechariah 4." *CBQ* 63, no.3 (2001): 430-443.

Bullock, C. Hassell. "Ezekiel, Bridge between the Testaments." *JETS* 25 (1982): 23-31.

Cameron, George G. "Darius, Egypt, and the 'Lands beyond the Sea.'" *JNES* 2, no.4 (1943): 307-313.

Campbell, J.C. "God's People and the Remnant." *SJT* 3 (1950): 78-85.

Carroll, Robert P. "Eschatological Delay in the Prophetic Tradition?" *ZAW* 94 (1982): 47-57.

Casey, Maurice. "Where Wright is Wrong: A Critical Review of N.T. Wright's Jesus and the Victory of God." *JSNT* 69 (1998): 95-103.

Cataldo, Jeremiah. "Persian Policy and the Yehud Community during Nehemiah." *JSOT* 28, no.2 (2003): 131-143.

Cathey, Joseph. Review of *Haggai, Malachi,* by Richard A. Taylor and E. Ray Clendenen, *RevBL* 05 (2005): 1-6.

Chhetri, Chitra. "בקשׁ." *NIDOTTE,* 1:720-726. Grand Rapids: Zondervan, 1997.

Chisholm, Robert. "A Theology of Jeremiah and Lamentations." In *A Biblical Theology of the Old Testament.* edited by Roy B. Zuck, 341-363. Chicago: Moody Press, 1991.

__________. "בשׂר." *NIDOTTE,* 1:777-779. Grand Rapids: Zondervan, 1997.

Christensen, Duane L. "Impulse and Design in the Book of Haggai." *JETS* 35, no.4 (1992): 445-456.

Clark, David J. "Problems in Haggai 2.15-19." *BT* 34, no.4 (1983): 432-439.

Clements, R.E. "Jeremiah, Prophet of Hope." *RevExp* 78 (1981): 345-363.

__________. "The Messianic Hope in the Old Testament." *JSOT* 43 (1989): 3-19.

__________. "The Prophecies of Isaiah and the Fall of Jerusalem in 587 B.C." *VT* 30 (1980): 421-436.

__________. "The Unity of the Book of Isaiah." *Int* 36, no.2 (1982): 117-129.

Clines, David J.A. "Haggai's Temple, Constructed, Deconstructed, and Reconstructed." *SJOT* 7, no.1 (1993): 51-77.

Coggins, Richard J. "The Exile: History and Ideology." *ExpTim* 110 (1999): 389-393.

Colless, Brian E. "Cyrus the Persian as Darius the Mede in the Book of Daniel." *JSOT* 56 (1992): 113-126.

Conrad, Edgar W. "Messengers in Isaiah and the Twelve: Implications for Reading Prophetic Books." *JSOT* 91 (2000): 83-97.

__________. "The End of Prophecy and the Appearance of Angels/ Messengers in the Book of the Twelve." *JSOT* 73 (1997): 65-79.

Coppes, Leonard J. "נדב." *TWOT,* 2:554-555. Chicago: Moody Press, 1980.

__________. "קרב." *TWOT,* 2:811-813. Chicago: Moody Press, 1980.

Cothenet, E. "Influence d'Ézéchiel sur la Spiritualité de Qumrân." (The influence of Ezekiel on the spiritual [life] of Qumran). *RevQ* 13 (1988): 431-439.

Cross, Frank Moore. "A Reconstruction of the Judean Restoration." *JBL* (1975): 4-18.

Davies, W.D. "Paul and the People of Israel." *JSNT* 24 (1996): 4-39.

De Vries, Simon J. "Remembrance in Ezekiel." *Int* 16, (1962): 58-64.

Denninger, David. "דרש." *NIDOTTE,* 1:993-999. Grand Rapids: Zondervan, 1997.

Dray, Stephen. "Ezra: An Applied Overview." *Evan* 24, no.2 (2006): 34-37.

Dubberstein, Waldo H. "The Chronology of Cyrus and Cambyses." *AJSL* 55 (October 1938): 417-419.

Dumbrell, William J. "Kingship and Temple in the Postexilic Period." *RTR* 37, no.2 (May-August 1978): 33-42.

__________. "The Purpose of the Book of Chronicles." *JETS* 27, no.3 (1984): 257-266.

Ellison, Henry L. "The Prophecy of Jeremiah." *EvQ* 31 (1959): 143-151.

Eskenazi, Tamara C. "Exile and the Dreams of Return." *CurTM* 17 (1990): 192-200.

Evans, Craig. "Jesus & the Continuing Exile of Israel." In *Jesus & the Restoration of Israel: A Critical Assessment of N.T. Wright's Jesus and the Victory of God,* ed. Carey C. Newman, 77-98. Downers Grove: InterVarsity, 1999.

__________. "Isa 6:9-13 in the Context of Isaiah's Theology." *JETS* 29, no.2 (1986): 139-146.

Ferguson, John. "The Remnant." *ExpTim* 99, no.1 (1987): 19-20.

Fishbane, Michael. "Sin and Judgment in the Prophecies of Ezekiel." *Int* 38, no.2 (2004): 130-150.

Floyd, Michael H. "The Evil in the Ephah: Reading Zechariah 5:5-11 in Its Literary Context." *CBQ* 58 (1996): 51-68.

__________. "Zechariah and Changing Views of Second Temple Judaism in Recent Commentaries." *RelSRev* 25 (1999): 257-263.

Fournier-Bidoz, Alain. "Des Mains de Zorobabel aux Yeux du Seigneur: Pour une Lecture Unitaire de Zacharie IV 1-14." (The hands of Zerubbabel in the eyes of the Lord: for reading Zechariah 4:1-14 as [a single] unit). *VT* 47 (1997): 537-542.

Fox, Michael V. "The Rhetoric of Ezekiel's Vision of the Valley of the Bones." *HUCA* 51 (1980): 1-15.

Freedman, David Noel. "Son of Man, Can These Bones Live?" *Int* 29 (1975): 171-186.

Fretheim, Terence E. "Is Anything Too Hard for God? (Jeremiah 32:27)." *CBQ* 66 (2004): 231-236.

Fried, Lisbeth S. "The House of the God Who Dwells in Jerusalem." *JAOS* 126, no.1 (2006): 89-102.

Gillingham. Sue. "From Liturgy to Prophecy: The Use of Psalmody in Second Temple Judaism." *CBQ* 64 (2002): 470-489.

Good, Robert M. "Zechariah's Second Night Vision (Zech 2:1-4)." *Bib* 63, no.1 (1982): 56-59.

Gosse, Bernard. "La Nouvelle Alliance et les Promesses d'Avenir se Referant à David dans les Livres de Jérémie, Ezéchiel, et Esaïe." (The New Covenant and Future Promises in Reference to David in the Books of Jeremiah, Ezekiel, and Isaiah). *VT* 41, no.4 (1991): 419-428.

Goulder, M. "Behold My Servant Jehoiachin." *VT* 53, no.2 (2002): 175-190.

Goulder, M.D. "The Songs of Ascents and Nehemiah." *JSOT* 75 (1997): 43-58.

Grisanti, Michael A. "חדה." *NIDOTTE*, 2:24-25. Grand Rapids: Zondervan, 1997.

__________. "שׁושׁ." *NIDOTTE*, 3:1223-1226. Grand Rapids: Zondervan, 1997.

Hallock, Richard T. "The 'One Year' of Darius I." *JNES* 19, no.1 (1960): 36-39.

Hamerton-Kelly, R.G. "The Temple and the Origins of Jewish Apocalyptic." *VT* 20 (1970): 1-15.

Hamilton, Victor P. "זרק." *NIDOTTE*, 1:1153-4. Grand Rapids: Zondervan, 1997.

__________. "עור." *NIDOTTE*, 3:357-360. Grand Rapids: Zondervan, 1997.

__________. "שׁכן." *TWOT*, 2:925-926. Chicago: Moody Press, 1980.

Hanson, Paul D. "Israelite Religion in the Early Postexilic Period." *Ancient Israelite Religion*. Philadelphia: Fortress Press (1987): 485-515.

Hartley, John E. "יתד." *TWOT*, 1:418-419. Chicago: Moody Press, 1980.

Hayes, John H. "The Tradition of Zion's Inviolability." *JBL* 82 (1963): 419-426.

Hellerman, Joseph. "Purity and Nationalism in Second Temple Literature: 1-2 Maccabees and *Jubilees*." *JETS* 46, no.3 (2003): 401-21.

Helyer, Larry R. "The Necessity, Problems, and Promise of Second Temple Judaism for Discussions of New Testament Eschatology." *JETS* 47, no.4 (2004): 597-615.

Hildebrand, David R. "Temple Ritual: A Paradigm for Moral Holiness in Haggai II 10-19." *VT* 39, no.2 (1989): 154-168.

Himmelfarb, Martha. "'A Kingdom of Priests': The Democratization of the Priesthood in the Literature of Second Temple Judaism." *JJTP* 6 (1997): 89-104.

Honeycutt, Roy L. "Jeremiah and the Cult." *RevExp* 58 (1961): 464-473.

House, Paul R. "Plot, Prophecy, and Jeremiah." *JETS* 36, no.3 (1993): 297-306.

Hubbard, David A. "Hope in the Old Testament." *TynBul* 34 (1983): 33-59.

Hustad, Donald P. "The Psalms as Worship Expression: Personal and Congregational." *RevExp* 81 (1984): 407-424.

James, Fleming. "Thoughts on Haggai and Zechariah." *JBL* 111 (1934): 229-235.

James, Peter. "Review of The Assyrian, Babylonian and Persian Periods in Palestine." *BAIAS* 22 (2004): 47-58.

Janowski, Bernd. "The One God of the Two Testaments." *ThTo* 57 (2000): 297-324.

Janzen, David. "The 'Mission' of Ezra and the Persian-Period Temple Community." *JBL* 119, no.4 (2000): 619-643.

__________. "Politics, Settlement, and Temple Community in Persian-Period Yehud." *CBQ* 64 (2002): 490-510.

Japhet, Sara. "Sheshbazzar and Zerubbabel—Against the Background of the Historical and Religious Tendencies of Ezra-Nehemiah." *ZAW* 94 (1982): 66-98.

Jenson, Philip P. "אהד." *NIDOTTE,* 1:349-351. Grand Rapids: Zondervan, 1997.

Jones, Ivor H. "Disputed Questions in Biblical Studies: 4. Exile and Eschatology." *ExpTim* 112 (2001): 401-405.

Jonker, Louis. "קרא." *NIDOTTE,* 3:971-974. Grand Rapids: Zondervan, 1997.

Kaiser, Walter C. Jr. "The Old Promise and the New Covenant: Jeremiah 31: 31-34." *JETS* 15 (1972): 11-23.

Kee, Min Suc. "The Heavenly Council and its Type-scene." *JSOT* 31, no.3 (2007): 259-273.

Kent, Roland G. "Old Persian Texts." *JNES* 2, no.2 (1943): 105-114.

Kessler, John A. "Building the Second Temple: Questions of Time, Text, and History in Haggai 1.1-15." *JSOT* 27, no.2 (2002): 243-256.

__________. "The Shaking of the Nations: An Eschatological View." *JETS* 30, no.2 (1987): 159-166.

King, Greg A. "The Remnant in Zephaniah." *BSac* 151 (Oct.-Dec. 1994): 414-427.

Kline, Meredith G. "The Structure of the Book of Zechariah." *JETS* 34, no.2 (1991): 179-193.

Kohn, Risa Levitt. "A New Heart and a New Soul: Ezekiel, the Exile and the Torah." *JSOT* Supplement Series *358*, (2002): 1-118.

Konkel, A.H. "חפש." *NIDOTTE*, 4:326-327. Grand Rapids: Zondervan, 1997.

Kuhrt, Amélie. "The Cyrus Cylinder and Achaemenid Imperial Policy." *JSOT* 25 (1983): 83-97.

Kvarme, Ole Chr. M. "Torah and Christ: On the Use of the Old Testament in the Early Synagogue and in the Early Church." *EvRT* 8, no.2 (1984): 183-201.

Lambert, David. "Did Israel Believe that Redemption Awaited Its Repentance? The Case of *Jubilees* 1." *CBQ* 68 (2006): 631-650.

Laperrousaz, Ernest-Marie. "Le Régime Théocratique Juif a-t-il Commencé à l'Epoque Perse, ou seulement à l'Epoque Hellénistique?" (Did the Jewish Theocratic Governance begin during the Persian Period or only during the Hellenistic Period?). *Sem* 32 (1982): 93-96.

Lemaire, A. "Les Inscriptions de Khribet El-Qôm et l'Ashérah de YHWH." (The Inscriptions from Khribet El-Qôm and the Asherah of YHWH). *RB* 85 (1977): 595-606.

Levenson, Jon D. "The Last Four Verses in Kings." *JBL* 103, no.3 (1984): 353-361.

__________. "The Temple and the World." *JR* 64, no.3 (1984): 275-298.

Lipiński, E. "Recherches sur the Livre de Zacharie." (Research on the book of Zechariah) *VT* 20 (1970): 25-55.

Lipton, Diana. "Early Mourning? Petitionary Versus Posthmous Ritual in Ezekiel XXIV." *VT* 56, no.2 (2006): 185-202.

Long, Burke O. "Reports of Visions among the Prophets." *JBL* 95, no.3 (1976): 353-65.

Luc, Alex. "A Theology of Ezekiel: God's Name and Israel's History." *JETS* 26, no.2 (1983): 137-143.

MacDonald, William. "Temple Theology." *Pneuma* 1 (1979): 39-48.

Mackay, Cameron. "Zechariah in Relation to Ezekiel 40-48." *EvQ* 40 (1968): 197-210.

Mantel, Hugo. "The Dichotomy of Judaism during the Second Temple." *HUCA* 44 (1973): 55-87.

Marsh, Clive. "Theological History? N.T. Wright's *Jesus and the Victory of God*." *JSNT* 69 (1998): 77-94.

Martens, Elmer A. "Accessing Theological Readings of a Biblical Book." *AUSS* 34, no.2 (1996): 223-237.

Mason, R.A. "Some Echoes of the Preaching in the Second Temple?" *ZAW* 96 (1984): 221-235.

__________. "The Purpose of the 'Editorial Framework' of the Book of Haggai." *VT* 27 (1976): 413-421.

May, Herbert Gordon. "A Key to the Interpretation of Zechariah's Visions." *JBL* 57, no.2 (1938): 173-184.

__________. "'This People' and 'This Nation' in Haggai." *VT* 18 (1968): 190-197.

McCartney, Dan G. "*Ecce Homo:* The Coming of the Kingdom as the Restoration of Human Vicegerency." *WTJ* 56 (1994): 1-21.

McConville, J.G. "Ezra-Nehemiah and the Fulfillment of Prophecy. *VT* 36, no.2 (1986): 205-224.

__________. "God's 'Name' and God's 'Glory.'" *TynBul* 29 (1978): 149-163.

McEntire, Mark. "Haggai—Bringing God into the Picture." *RevExp* 97 (2000): 69-78.

McEvenue, Sean E. "The Political Structure in Judah from Cyrus to Nehemiah." *CBQ* 43 (1981): 353-364.

McKeating, H. "Ezekiel the 'Prophet Like Moses?" *JSOT* 61 (1994): 97-109.

Merrill, Eugene H. "Remembering: A Central Theme in Biblical Worship." *JETS* 43, no.1 (2000): 27-36.

Meyers, Eric M. "The Use of *tôrâ* in Haggai 2:11 and the Role of the Prophet in the Restoration Community." In *The Word of the Lord Shall Go Forth,* eds. Carol L. Meyers and M. O'Connor, 69-76. Winona Lake: Eisenbrauns, 1983.

Millard, Alan R. "Approaching the Old Testament." *Them* (1977): 34-39.

Miller, John H. "Haggai—Zechariah: Prophets of the Now and Future." *CurTM* 6, no.2 (1979): 99-104.

Morgenstern, Julian. "Two Prophecies from 520-516 B.C." *HUCA* 22, no.1 (1949): 376-427.

Mowvley, Harry. "The Concept and Content of 'Blessing' in the Old Testament." *BT* 16, no.2 (1965): 74-80.

Mulzac, Kenneth D. "The Remnant and the New Covenant in the Book of Jeremiah." *AUSS* 34, no.2 (1996): 239-248.

__________ "'The Remnant of My Sheep': A Study of Jeremiah 23:1-8 in its Biblical and Theological Contexts." *JATS* 13, no.1 (2002):134-148.

Murphy, Ronald E. "Once Again—The 'Center' of the Old Testament." *BTB* 31, no.3 (2001): 85-89.

Murray, Donald F. "Of all the Years the Hopes—or Fears? Jehoiachin in Babylon (2 Kings 25:27-30)." *JBL* 120, no.2 (2001): 245-265.

Nakarai, Toyozo W. "Worship in the Old Testament." *Enc* 34 (1973): 282-286.

Niditch, Susan. "Ezekiel 40-48 in a Visionary Context." *CBQ* 48, no.2 (2004): 208-215.

Ollenburger, Ben C. "Discoursing Old Testament Theology." *BibInt* 11 (2003): 617-628.

__________. "The Book of Zechariah." *NIB*, vol. 7, edited by Leander E. Keck, 735-840. Nashville: Abingdon Press, 1996.

O'Brien, Julia M. "Nahum—Habakkuk—Zephaniah: Reading the 'Former Prophets' in the Persian Period." *Int* 169 (2007): 168-183.

Olmstead, A.T. "Darius as Lawgiver." *AJSL* 51, no.4 (1935): 247-249.

Olyan, Saul M. "'We are Utterly Cut Off': Some Possible Nuances of לנו נגזרנו in Ezek 37:11." *CBQ* 65 (2003):43-51.

Oswalt, John N. "The Book of Isaiah: A Short Course in Biblical Theology." *CTJ* 39 (2004): 54-71.

__________. "בכה." *TWOT,* 1:107-108. Chicago: Moody Press, 1980.

__________. "ברך." *TWOT,* 1:132-133. Chicago: Moody Press, 1980.

Owens, John J. "Jeremiah, Prophet of True Religion." *RevExp* 78 (1981): 365-378.

Parker, Richard A. "Darius and His Egyptian Campaign." *AJSL* 58, no.4 (1941): 373-377.

Pearce, Laurie E. "New Evidence for Judeans in Babylonia." In *Judah and the Judeans in the Persian Period.* Winona Lake: Eisenbrauns (2006): 399-411.

"Persian Susa." *BAR* 23, no.1 (1997): 80.

Petersen, David L. Zechariah's Visions: A Theological Perspective." *VT* 34, no.2 (1984): 195-206.

__________. "Zerubbabel and Jerusalem Temple Reconstruction." *CBQ* 36, no.3 (1974): 366-372.

Petitjean, A. "La Mission de Zorobabel et la Reconstruction du Temple." (Zerubbabel's Mission and the Rebuilding of the Temple). *ETL* 42, no.1 (1966): 40-71.

Pierce, Ronald W. "A Thematic Development of the Haggai/Zechariah/Malachi Corpus." *JETS* 27, no.4 (1984): 401-411.

Poebel, Arno. "Chronology of Darius' First year of Reign." *AJSL* 55, no.2 (1938): 142-165.

Polaski, Donald C. "Reflections on the Mosaic Covenant: The Eternal Covenant (Isaiah 24.5) and Intertextuality." *JSOT* 77 (1998): 55-73.

Potter, H.D. "The New Covenant in Jeremiah XXXI 31-34." *VT* 33, no.3 (1983): 347-357.

Pyne, Robert A. "The 'Seed,' the Spirit, and the Blessing of Abraham." *BSac* 152 (April-June 1995): 211-222.

Quarles, Charles L. "The New Perspective and Means of Atonement in Jewish Literature of the Second Temple Period." *CTR* 2 (Spring 2005): 39-56.

Redditt, Paul. "Themes in Haggai—Zechariah—Malachi." *Int* 61 (2007): 184-197.

__________. "Zerubbabel, Joshua, and the Night Visions of Zechariah." *CBQ* 54, no.2 (1992): 249-259.

Reiss, Moshe. "Jeremiah, the Suffering Prophet, and Ezekiel, the Visionary." *JBQ* 32, no.4 (2004): 233-238.

Richards, Kent H. "Reflections on a New Haggai Commentary." *IR* (Spring 1985): 38-42.

Roberts, J.J.M. "Isaiah in Old Testament Theology." *Int* 36 (1982): 130-143.

__________. "The Hand of Yahweh." *VT* 21 (1971): 244-251.

Rom-Shiloni, Dalit. "Facing Destruction and Exile: Inner-Biblical Exegesis in Jeremiah and Ezekiel." *ZAW* 117 (2005): 189-205.

Roukema, Riemer. "Herman Ridderbos's Redemptive-Historical Exegesis of the New Testament." *WTJ* 66, (2004): 259-73.

Rudman, Dominic. "Zechariah 5 and the Priestly Law." *SJOT* 14 (2000): 194-206.

Saucy, Robert L. "A Rationale for the Future of Israel." *JETS* 28 (1985): 433-442.

Schaper, Joachim. "The Jerusalem Temple as an Instrument of the Achaemenid Fiscal Administration." *VT* 45, no.4 (1995): 528-539.

Schenker, Adrien. "L'Origine de l'Idée d'une Alliance entre Dieu et Israél dans l'Ancien Testament." (The Origin of the Idea of a Covenant between God and Israel in the Old Testament). *RB* 95 (1988): 184-194.

Schiffman, Lawrence H. "The Concept of the Messiah in Second Temple and Rabbinic Literature." *RevExp* 84, no.2 (1987): 235-246.

Schöpflin, Karin. "The Composition of Metaphorical Oracles within the Book of Ezekiel." *VT* 55, no.1 (2005): 101-120.

Scobie, Charles H.H. "Israel and the Nations: An Essay in Biblical Theology." *TynBul* 43, no.2 (1992): 283-305.

Seitz, Christopher R. "The Crisis of Interpretation over the Meaning and Purpose of the Exile." *VT* 35 (1985): 78-97.

__________. "The Divine Council, Temporal Transition, and New Prophecy in the Book of Isaiah." *JBL* 109, no.2 (1990): 229-247.

Simcox, Carroll E. "The Role of Cyrus in Deutero-Isaiah." *JAOS* 57, no.2 (1937): 158-171.

Sklba, Richard J. "'Until the Spirit from on High is Poured out on Us' (Isa 32:15): Reflections on the role of the Spirit in the Exile." *CBQ* 46, no.1 (2006): 1-10.

Smick, Elmer B. "ברית." *TWOT*, 1:128-130. Chicago: Moody Press, 1980.

Smiles, Vincent M. "The Concept of 'Zeal' in Second-Temple Judaism and Paul's Critique of It in Romans 10:2." *CBQ* 64, no.2 (2002): 282-299.

Spieckermann, H. "God's Steadfast Love: Towards a New Conception of Old Testament Theology." *Bib* 81 (2000): 305-327.

Stager, Lawrence E. "Climatic Conditions and Grain Storage in the Persian Period." *HTR* 64 (October 1971): 448-450.

Staples, W.E. "The 'Soul' in the Old Testament." *AJSL* 44, no.3 (1928): 145-176.

Stern, Ephraim. "The Material Culture of the Phoenicians." *BA* 56, no.3 (1993): 135-137.

__________. "The Religious Revolution in Persian-Period Judah." In *Judah and the Judeans in the Persian Period*. Winona Lake: Eisenbrauns (2006): 199-205.

Talley, David. "חפץ." *NIDOTTE*, 2:231-234. Grand Rapids: Zondervan, 1997.

Taylor, Barnard C. "The Divine Names as They Occur in the Prophets." *Heb* 2, no.2 (1886):109-110.

Taylor, Joan E. "A Second Temple in Egypt: The Evidence for the Zadokite Temple of Onias." *JSJ* 29, no.3 (1998): 297-321.

Thompson, J.A. and Elmer A. Martens, "שוב." *NIDOTTE*, 4:55-59. Grand Rapids: Zondervan, 1997.

Torrey, Charles C. "Medes and Persians." *JAOS* 66, no.1 (1946):1-15.

Trotter, James. "Was the Second Jerusalem Temple a Primarily Persian Project?" *SJOT* 15, no.2 (2001): 276-294.

Tuell, Steven S. "Ezekiel 40-42 as Verbal Icon." *CBQ* 58 (1996): 649-664.

Unvala, J.M. "The Palace of Darius the Great and the Apadana of Artaxerxes II in Susa." *BSOS, University of London* 5, no.2 (1929): 229-232.

Van Dam, Cornelis. "בדל." *NIDOTTE,* 1:603-605. Grand Rapids: Zondervan, 1997.

Vanderkam, James C. "Joshua the High Priest and the Interpretation of Zechariah 3." *CBQ* 53, no.4 (1991): 553-571.

Van Winkle, D.W. "The Relationship of the Nations to Yahweh and to Israel in Isaiah XL-LV." *VT* 35, no.4 (1985): 447-458.

Verhoef, Pieter A. "חדש." *NIDOTTE,* 2:30-37. Grand Rapids: Zondervan, 1997.

Vincent, Jean Marcel. "L'Apport de la Recherche Historique et ses Limites pour la Compréhension de Visions Nocturnes de Zacharie." (The Contribution of Historic Research and its Limits in Understanding Zechariah's Night Visions). *Bib* 87, no.1 (2006): 22-41.

Walton, John H. "Vision Narrative Wordplay and Jeremiah XXIV." *VT* 39, no.4 (1989): 508-509.

Watts, James W. "The Remnant Theme: A Survey of New Testament Research, 1921-1987." *PRSt* 15, no.2 (1988): 109-129.

Watts, John D.W. "Jeremiah—A Character Study." *RevExp* 58 (1961): 428-437.

Whitelam, Keith W. "Recreating the History of Israel." *JSOT* 35 (1986): 45-70.

Williamson, Hugh G.M. "The Governors of Judah under the Persians." *TynBul* 39 (1988): 59-82.

Wilson, Robert R. "An Interpretation of Ezekiel's Dumbness." *VT* 22, (1972): 91-104.

Wolf, Herbert. "'The Desire of All Nations' in Haggai 2:7: Messianic or Not?" *JETS* 19, no.2 (1976): 97-102.

__________. "זמם." *TWOT,* 1:244-245. Chicago: Moody Press, 1980.

Wong, G.C.I. "A Note on 'Joy' in Nehemiah VIII 10." *VT* 45, no.3 (1995): 383-85.

Wright, N.T. "Theology, History and Jesus: A Response to Maurice Casey and Clive Marsh." *JSNT* 69 (1998): 105-112.

Youngblood, Ronald F. "תאנה." *TWOT,* 2:963. Chicago: Moody Press, 1980.

Zimmer, Robert G. "The Temple of God." *JETS* 18 (1975): 41-46.

Zimmerli, Walther. "The Message of the Prophet Ezekiel." *Int* vol.23, no.2 (1969): 131-157.

CPSIA information can be obtained at www.ICGtesting.com
Printed in the USA
LVOW12s2336190913

353252LV00002B/269/P